Foreword by
Don Yaeger
Seven-Time New York Times Bestselling Author

THE

POWER

OF

STORYTELLING

THE ART OF INFLUENTIAL COMMUNICATION

TY BENNETT

The Power of Storytelling
Sound Concepts, Inc.
782 S Auto Mall Dr., Suite A
American Fork, Utah 84003

For additional copies of this book please visit
www.increaseinfluence.com or www.SoundConcepts.com

No information contained herein is meant to replace the advice of a
doctor or healthcare practitioner. The data and opinions appearing in
this book are for informational purposes only. Readers are encouraged
to seek advice from qualified health professionals.

ISBN 978-1-933057-72-9

Advanced Praise for The Power of Storytelling

"Stories are the effective communicator's most powerful tool. To lead, sell and communicate, you must engage and educate through the stories you tell. You can learn how to be a master storyteller from this new book by Ty Bennett. He's made it easy to understand how to lead, influence and move others by crafting and delivering memorable stories."

- **Mark Sanborn,** Acclaimed Speaker and bestselling author of *The Fred Factor and You Don't Need a Title to be a Leader*

"The science and power of storytelling is revealed, and how you can adapt that power to your career. Facts and figures are forgotten. Stories are retold."

- **Jeffrey Gitomer,** author of *The Little Red Book of Selling*

"A compelling story is like music in a noisy world: it makes us want to stop and listen. [A must-read for network marketers,] The Power of Storytelling will help you practice and master this ancient art."

- **Dr. Josephine Gross,** Editor in Chief, *Networking Times*

"Ty Bennett articulates Plato's quote: "Those who tell the stories, rule the world." Ty teaches the power of storytelling in all the environments and mediums we encounter and have access to. Thank you Ty for reinforcing the need to use an art form that is getting lost in the minutia and that is to be able to tell a great story at the right time, the right way to engage and influence your audience."

- **David K. Williams,** Forbes and HBR columnist and Author of *The 7 Non Negotiables of Winning,* CEO of Nationally recognized Fishbowl

"In their award-wining 'New York Times' best-seller 'Influencer'— The Power To Change Anything, the authors' research proved beyond doubt the persuasive power of stories. But they didn't tell us how to create and craft them. That's where Ty Bennett 'white-knight's it' by drilling down into the bolts & nuts of making and delivering memorable and compelling stories that move people to take the actions we want them to. This is an uber-useful book!"

- **John Milton Fogg,** author of *The Greatest Networker in the World*

"There I sat with an inbox full of messages and a colleague's new book to read before my plane on Monday morning. It would have been easy to postpone the reading but the title intrigued me, "Storytelling", and I thought, "I may be able to use some of these ideas in my speech on Tuesday." So I started to read it. Immediately it grabbed my attention. How? By telling me a story of course, and then explaining why that works so well. By the time I looked up at my clock I had read the entire book. Now I understand why my own stories have worked so well over the years, and I know how to make them even better. You will too. Read this book now!"

- **Jim Cathcart,** CSP, CPAE author of *Relationship Selling* and *The Acorn Principle*

"To influence others, being a storyteller is a must. Ty has distilled the art and science of being a great storyteller into a fast and fun read. We highly recommend this book!"

- **Richard Fenton & Andrea Waltz,** Authors, *Go for No!*

"A great primer to hone your craft of storytelling, to increase your influence."

- **Randy Gage,** Author of the New York Times bestseller, *Risky Is the New Safe*

"Ty Bennett has mastered the ART of storytelling. His diligence in defining a story's mechanics, with vast experience in the field of sales and communication, all packaged in one HOW-TO guide to creating your most influential existence makes Ty one of the Leaders of his craft. Buy this book! It will change the way you teach your children, give your speech on stage, and sell anything."

-**Jason Hewlett,** Award Winning Entertainer and Inspirational Speaker

"Whether we're convincing our kids to eat dinner, our bosses to raise our salaries, or our customers to buy our products, storytelling is the heart of how we communicate. To create compelling narratives that inspire and enlighten, devour Ty's book!"

- **Ruby Newell-Legner,** Fan Experience Expert, Author of *7 Star Service Culture*

"Ty Bennett adds value to everything and everyone he touches! His book will help you increase your ability to influence and motivate others to take action. Sales is your number one business skill and Ty helps you master it!"

- **Tiffany Peterson,** Speaker & Coach, *The Lighthouse Principles*

"I attribute my success in business to one single component – the ability to tell a good story. It has served me well on the stage, on the page, in my marketing, my sales calls, and my ability to influence those around me. If you want to hold the key to reaching a higher level of impact, I highly recommend that you read Ty's book."

- **Kelly Swanson,** Award-Winning Storyteller, Motivational Speaker, and Author of *Who Hijacked My Fairy Tale?*

"From the tales told around the campfires of our most ancient ancestors to the texts zapped to today's digital screens, storytelling is the key to human communication and persuasion. Ty Bennett's fascinating new book will help you turn your storytelling into story selling."

- **Bruce Turkel,** Branding expert and author of *Building Brand Value*

CONTENTS

FOREWORD

As a young boy, I couldn't wait for the mail delivery on Wednesday to receive Sports Illustrated. But it wasn't just that I loved sports; I loved the stories that made everything come to life. For years I made that trek to the mailbox knowing that the storytelling within those pages would take me places I could only imagine. Though the magazine was well known for its extraordinary photography, I was taken by the words. A budding writer, I would read those stories always asking myself what creative genius had allowed the writers to put words together in a way that painted such vivid pictures.

From that experience I started studying the art of storytelling. I wanted to know how I, too, could make my writing AND my conversation more compelling, more real. The study took me many places – I took classes, sought mentors, read about the art – and eventually, that study took me to Sports Illustrated, where for a dozen years I worked as Staff Writer and Associate Editor with the magazine.

Working arm in arm with the best storytellers in the world, I watched their attention to detail. I learned how to use those details to bring any reader or audience member right into the room with you when sharing an event. I learned what it meant to get the listener or reader to become an active participant in the story, which both enhances their experience and increases the memorability of your presentation. The highest compliment, obviously, was to tell stories that others would repeat. Even greater, though, would be to tell stories that they could repeat with a high level of accuracy because your description had been so engaging that they couldn't help but remember the tale.

I began applying these lessons to everything I wrote, including my work as an author. I've now penned nearly two dozen books and had seven of them become New York Times Best-sellers. In each book, I work with my editors to hone stories that create a page-turning experience. Though all of my books are non-fiction, I want the words to pull a reader along just as effectively as Nicholas Sparks or John Grisham.

In 2008 I took an early retirement from Sports Illustrated to begin a second career as a professional speaker. I hired coaches to help me as I learned how to apply many of these storytelling tips to the stage. Had I met him then, Ty Bennett would have been one of my coaches! Ty knows that all of us are filled with stories … but only some of us tell them in ways that change the way others listen.

The lessons Ty brings you here are powerful. He works on establishing your platform from the first word to the last, creating a storytelling quilt that wraps the audience. As I read his work, listened to his lessons I found myself stopping often to make notes in the margins and think about how everything I do can be more impactful. I found myself looking for ways to tighten what I do to make every word matter.

It doesn't matter what line of work you are currently mastering – from sales to management to coaching to speaking – you will achieve more as you learn the art of storytelling. It is the most powerful form of communication available to us and you will be grateful that you chose to improve yourself and accelerate your career by reading this book.

Be Great!

Don Yaeger

Author of *Greatness: 16 Characteristics of True Champions*

MY STORY

Chapter 1

MY STORY

"The universe is made of stories, not of atoms."
– Muriel Rukeyser

Have you ever met one of your heroes?

As a speaker and as an author Dr. Stephen Covey is one of my heroes. Not only was Dr. Covey named one of the 100 Most Influential People of the 21st Century by *Time Magazine,* his book *The Seven Habits Of Highly Effective People* was named the No. 1 business book of the 21st Century.

I had a chance to meet Dr. Stephen Covey a few years ago at an event he hosted in his home. A mutual friend introduced us by saying, "Stephen, this is Ty Bennett, he's writing a book." Stephen asked, "What is your book about Ty?" I replied, "It is about communication and influence."

He said, "That's great, can I give you some advice?" His book has sold about 26 million copies! Without hesitation I said, "I would love your advice."

He said, "Make sure you write your book for the reader and not the writer." I asked, "What do you mean by that?" He said, "A book that's written for the writer, to build him up, to make him successful, will never achieve what it desires. A book that's written for the reader, to teach, to inspire, to help, will make an impact." He continued, "it's much more about contribution than achievement."

From the outset, I want you to know that this book was written for you—the reader. I wrote *The Power of Storytelling* to teach you the most influential form of communication. It is a skill that has helped me succeed and I know will help you succeed as well.

If you are reading this book, then I am going to assume that you are an influencer. I define an influencer as anyone involved in speaking, selling, leading or teaching. And every influencer I know is constantly asking some variation on these essential questions: How do I communicate in a more concise, compelling, influential manner? And how do I cause people to adopt my ideas, buy my products, remember my message or take action?

When I was twenty-one years old, my brother Scott and I started a business together. I quickly discovered that I didn't have a lot of credibility when it came to influencing others. We had marginal success but not the kind we were after. So I started to study communication and influence. I read books, attended seminars, listened to audio programs, and practiced what I learned. Through my study I found some keys to how to tell my story and communicate my message that caused people to listen and to eventually follow me. We ended up building that business to over $20 million dollars in annual revenue while still in our twenties. I since have had a chance to share my influence strategies, as a speaker and author, with hundreds of thousands of people around the world.

What I've discovered is that when it comes to communicating with others, most speakers, leaders, teachers, and coaches are striving for perfection in their message, when what they should be worried about is connection. The interesting thing is that we forget the fundamental basic of how humans connect:

People respond based on emotion.

We've all heard that before, but what does it mean? It means that the first level of response to any communication will be in accordance to how it makes the listener feel. It's the audience's emotional reaction that creates connection, causes engagement, stimulates learning, solidifies memory, and causes them to take action. That is why Peter Guber said, "Move your listeners' hearts and their feet and wallet will follow."

As an influencer, how then do you stimulate emotion? Here are a few questions to think about:

- Are you selling intellectually or emotionally?
- Are you casting your vision with just facts and statistics and missing the opportunity to make an emotional connection?
- Are your speeches and presentations death by power point or are you engaging your audience?

Anyone who hopes to connect with another human being needs to learn to communicate emotionally. So how do we do that?

The answer is the subject of this book. Stories.

People love stories. Stories inspire, stories motivate—
stories evoke emotion in people that causes them to
respond, to take action, to adopt your ideas, and buy
your products. Robert McKee put it well when he said,
"Storytelling is the most powerful way to put ideas into the
world today"

Stories are an influencer's best friend. If you are involved
in speaking, selling, leading or teaching, then storytelling
is a communication and influence strategy you need to
master. This book will help you do just that.

I have taught this material to thousands of influencers
through keynotes, workshops, webinars, and conference
calls. These influencers include professional speakers,
executives, politicians, pastors, network marketers,
financial planners, teachers, and salespeople. Now I am
laying it all out in *The Power of Storytelling.*

The book is divided into three sections:
1. Mindset
2. Skillset
3. Toolset

In the first section you are going to learn how to think like an influencer. Your mindset is critical because understanding the psychology and science makes the techniques of storytelling both reflexive and effective.

The skills necessary to deliver an influential story are something anyone can learn and acquire, and I will teach you the structure and secrets to perfect your storytelling. Here is the key, though: your perfection will come outside of this book as you practice and apply what is being taught.

I believe what Nancy Mellon said, "Because there is a natural storytelling urge and ability in all human beings, even just a little nurturing of this impulse can bring about astonishing and delightful results."

In the second section you will learn about the toolset that makes stories come alive. These are specific techniques that you can apply within your stories to make them more compelling, more dynamic, and more memorable.

Inside each chapter you will find Expert Tips and Expert Examples. The Expert Tips will provide additional insight into the concepts being taught. The Expert Examples are stories that I use to illustrate a concept. Many of these stories include links to a video where you can see the story being told. I have found video to be a powerful teaching method for storytelling. You can simply type the video link into a web browser. You can access all of the videos on the youtube channel – www.youtube.com/storytellingbook

CLIMB IN THE WHEELBARROW

One of the great places to find stories is from history. In the mid 1800s there was a famous tightrope walker from France who was known as The Great Blondin. In 1855, The Great Blondin made the trip to New York to join a traveling show. It was there that he came up with the idea that would make him famous.

The Great Blondin ran an1,100 foot rope across the gorge at Niagara Falls, 160 feet above the water, and attempted to cross it. (Can you imagine?)

On June 30, 1859 he successfully crossed Niagara Falls. News traveled quickly and he soon had enormous crowds of people coming to watch this crazy act.

Never to be outdone, The Great Blondin soon began to add more to his act than simply walking across the rope. He crossed the falls once with his manager on his back. Another time he carried a rope on his shoulder to the middle of the falls, tied it on to the main rope, shimmied down and took a drink out of the water below, and then climbed back up and crossed the rest of the way. Another time he carried a chair to the middle, balanced one leg of the chair on the rope, and stood on top.

The Great Blondin was the greatest tightrope walker that ever lived.

Then one day after he crossed the falls, an old man pushing a wheelbarrow approached The Great Blondin and said, "Sir, I want you to push my wheelbarrow across the rope." The Great Blondin studied the man for a moment and replied, "I'll do it, but only if you climb in the wheelbarrow."

The man climbed in the wheelbarrow.

As you begin this book, I'll make you a deal. If you climb in the wheelbarrow, I'll take you across. What does it mean to climb in the wheelbarrow? It means that you are not just going to read this book, you are going to study its content. It means that you are going to practice these techniques to make your storytelling powerful. It means you are committed.

Climb in the wheelbarrow, and I will take you across the rope.

(By the way, that is an example of using a story to teach a point)

SECTON ONE: MINDSET

"You can teach all the other stuff you know. You can teach shooting the ball, you can teach having a good touch, passing and whatnot, but when you get out there on the field, it's just a mindset you need to go in the game with."
—Freddy Adu, professional soccer player

The dictionary defines mindset as "a complex mental state involving beliefs and feelings and values and dispositions to act in certain ways."

Each of us has a mindset that affects the way we interact and communicate with others.

In this section we're going to talk about the mindset of an influencer being the precursor for all that follows. Understanding what mindset is and the role it plays is essential to success. If your mindset isn't in tune with your objective—if the beliefs and feelings and values and dispositions that create it are somehow not in sync with your goals—the most well-intentioned, well-crafted story can fall as flat and be rendered as ineffective as if it were never told at all.

Recognizing the importance of mindset will bring into focus how vital it is to hone the skills and utilize those tools that develop the right kind of mindset. Your skillset and toolset are what get you in the game, allowing your mindset to take over and let you perform as an effective storyteller and influencer.

UNDERSTANDING INFLUENCE

Chapter 2

UNDERSTANDING INFLUENCE

"It is not the voice that commands the story:
it is the ear."
– Italo Calvino

It's not about you—it's about them!

The focus of an influencer is always on the audience.

If you are a speaker—it's about the people listening to you.

If you are in sales—it's about your customer or prospect.

If you are a leader—it's about the people you are leading.

If you are a teacher—it's about your students.

Almost everyone has this backwards. They think being influential means they need to become polished or powerful. Influence, though, is all about the audience. Be it an audience of one or one thousand. When we make it about them, we grow in their eyes.

This is especially true in storytelling. If the audience doesn't see how your story pertains to them, they won't care. It could be the most well crafted story ever told and yet it will miss the mark unless you connect it to those to whom it is being delivered.

When I was 21 years old I was struggling as a young entrepreneur. I wasn't selling as much as I would like and I just couldn't seem to influence people. I kept asking myself, "Why won't people buy from me? Why am I not influential?"

The change started to happen when I began to look at things from my prospects' point of view; when I starting asking questions like, "What makes me want to follow and buy from someone else?"

Putting myself in the prospects' perspective allowed me to understand and, eventually, change the way I was doing things. I could see that the people who had the greatest influence on me, who compelled me to want to buy what they were selling, were those who took an interest in me, in what I wanted and needed. That kind of thinking turned everything around and I began to experience much greater success as a salesperson.

Learning to ask questions from the other perspective is a trait of the highly successful. A speaker shouldn't ask, "What do I want to share?" but rather, "What does the audience want/need to hear?" A teacher should look at things from the student's perspective. A manager should look at things from the team's perspective. A coach should look at things from the players' perspective.

If you are struggling to connect, influence or impact the way that you would desire, try taking a step back and looking at it from the other point of view.

YOUR PURPOSE

As an influencer your purpose is to do one thing: engage the audience.

What do you think it means to engage?

According to Webster's, to engage means to cause someone to be involved; to attract their attention; to engross them.

If you are teaching, leading, selling or speaking, your purpose is to engage your audience. Above all, you want to grab their attention and get them involved. Your prospect, client, customer, employee, team member, or student has to be engaged or they won't buy your product, act on your idea or implement your plan. Without engagement, there is no influence.

In the spirit of engagement, I believe that we should move from giving sales presentations to having sales conversations. There's a huge difference between the two. A sales presentation, by definition, is a monologue, while a sales conversation is a dialogue—it involves both parties and the emphasis is on the buyer, not the seller.

I know we have all done this before. We give a sales presentation (a monologue) and then at the end we ask, "Do you have any questions?"
There is nothing about that model that makes it about

the audience; nothing that makes them part of the conversation. For an actual conversation to take place, there needs to be interaction, back-and-forth talking, and listening. Remember, a great storyteller is first a great story listener.

I'm sure that many of you who speak, lead or teach don't view yourself as being in sales. The truth is, however, we are all in sales. Whether it's a product, a service, a vision, an idea, a strategy or ourselves that we are trying to promote, it is all sales. Embrace that principle, learn to sell effectively, and watch your influence grow exponentially.

Expert Tip: Great presenters learn to be interactive in their presentations. That doesn't mean people in the audience need to interrupt and speak during the presentation. Interaction and participation can come by way of laughter, rhetorical questions, taking notes, brainstorming ideas—the list goes on and on.

Not long ago, I had a chance to attend a conference of The National Speakers Association. While I was there I met many other speakers and the typical conversation started by someone asking, "What do you speak about?"

I replied to one particular lady, "I speak on influence to sales and leadership organizations."

She said, "So are you a sales speaker or a leadership speaker?" And I said, "Both."

She looked puzzled and responded, "You can't be both." I laughed and said, "Then I guess I'm in trouble because I am."

So how does this pertain to sales presentations versus sales conversations? I think that sales has changed. The old school approaches of push strategies, arm-twisting, and high pressure don't work anymore—if they ever did.

Sales today is about influence. It's about moving people.

Lisa Sasevich, a top sales trainer, said, "In today's world, people are looking to be inspired. Encouraged. Taught. Heard. It's no longer about simply selling. It's about becoming a trusted advisor. You're now learning to influence. And that, my friends, is where you begin to make the biggest impact and attract dedicated, highly committed, highly invested clients and contributors."

I completely agree with Lisa.

They say that leadership is influence. But here is the insight—so is sales. And while we are on the topic, so is speaking, marketing, teaching, and coaching. If you are in the people business (which we all are) then you need to learn to influence people.

Push strategies don't influence others, they turn people off and drive them away. They achieve the exact opposite of our purpose of engagement: grabbing their attention and getting them emotionally involved.

And that brings us back to stories.

The reason that stories are an influencer's best friend is because they are the ultimate pull strategy—the polar opposite of push. A pull strategy is about attraction, and stories naturally draw people in, causing them to listen, learn, and respond. When you share the right story, in the right manner, your message will become magnetic and you will increase your influential pull.

FIVE TOOLS OF ENGAGEMENT

Your purpose as a communicator is to engage your audience, pure and simple. So how do you do it? Here are five tools that will help you grab the attention of your audience and make them part of your conversation:

Tool Number One.
Making Your Message About Your Audience.

If you want to engage your audience then you need to start by making your message about them. The truth is nobody cares about your message, product, story or idea unless they see how it will benefit them in their life. President Theodore Roosevelt said, "Nobody cares how much you know until they know how much you care." Great influencers understand this and make their message irresistible because it is all about their audience.

There are two easy ways that you can do this:

1—Share a relatable analogy or experience.

If the analogies and experiences you use are easily understood by your audience—if they can relate to what you're saying— it will compel them to pay attention. When talking to a realtor about your product, make sure you use an analogy that they will connect with. If you are speaking to a group of mothers, then your college basketball experience is probably not your most relatable story. I know that this probably seems logical, but you would be amazed at how often people don't think about relating to their audience and instead just share what they want to say.

2—Use "You" and lose "I" and "Me."

Using "you" increases the audience's engagement in your speech. If we want to make our message about them, then we need to stop saying, me, me, me and I, I, I and start saying "you" statements and asking "you" focused questions. Let me give you an example: Which of these sentences is more engaging?

- Everyone has difficult times in their lives.

Or

- Have you ever had a difficult time in your life?

The second engages the listener emotionally and mentally because the word "you" draws them in.

Janelle Barlow, President of the Global Speakers Federation, did an analysis in 2008 of three speeches. The night that Barack Obama won the Democratic Primary, both Barack Obama and Hilary Clinton spoke, as well as John McCain. On that night Janelle found that Clinton and McCain said the word "I" in their speeches twice as much as Obama. We all know the outcome of the election now and in 2008 it was Obama's speeches that put him over the top. His ability to engage and persuade his audience started with his use of the word "you" and making it about them.

Tool Number Two. Questions.

Questions are the way that we turn our presentations into conversations. They create curiosity—causing the listener to want to know more. They compel the audience to reflect and to apply the message to their own experiences, their own lives. Learning to ask engaging questions is a skill that takes practice. When you are one on one, then your questions will solicit a response and create dialogue. When you are speaking to a group, your questions will cause the audience to reflect. As the speaker, you need to learn to give a pause after your questions so that the audience can have time to think.

This is an art because not enough pause tramples over their thought process, but too much pause is awkward. It takes practice. As was mentioned in Tool #1, your questions should be "you" focused questions. We will also learn more about this in Chapter 5 in the section: Bringing The Audience Into Your Story.

Tool Number Three. Humor.

Humor is a great engagement tool because it breaks down barriers between you and your audience, makes an immediate connection and increases your likeability. Humor can't be forced, however. I am not suggesting that you go into a presentation with a knock-knock joke prepared, but if we can get over our nerves and just be ourselves, we will start to add humor into our presentations, in context, that causes people to smile and makes us relatable. When it comes to storytelling, we don't need to add humor; we need to uncover it. There are funny things that happen in our interactions with people and humorous things that are said. Our job is to be aware and recognize those things and share them in our stories.

If you want to learn to add humor into your presentations and understand the formulas, techniques and tools that comedians use, I would recommend The Comedy Bible, by Judy Carter. The book is full of the templates and formulas to develop funny content and material. If you put them to work, they will add a lot of humor to your presentations.

Tool Number Four. Shock

A shocking statement can be intriguing and cause your audience to engage quickly. Controversy is compelling and if used correctly can be a great engagement tool.

There are many presenters who use controversy as their "stich." When every expert is saying, "It is this way," and you come out and say, "they are all wrong and it is really this way," your audience will be all ears. Controversy can grab people's attention and become a powerful attraction tool. If you use this approach you have to be able to back it up and convince people of your position, so it requires a high level of confidence and communication ability. The caution I would give with this approach is that I have seen people attempt to utilize this strategy when it is outside their personality. If you come across as inauthentic or fake, it will do more harm then good. But if you can pull it off, controversy is very engaging.

Tool Number Five. Stories.

We've been talking throughout the chapter about stories so it may come as a surprise to you to see stories listed as a tool. But the fact is, you can use all the other tools on this list and still not communicate with a story. In talking to an audience, you can make it about them, you can avoid talking with "I" and "me," you can use humor, you can deliver shock value—but it's when all these valuable tools are used in an effective, captivating, absorbing story that they become so much greater than the sum of their parts.

Throughout the rest of this book you will learn to tell stories that engage, persuade and inspire; stories that magnify memory, causing your audience to retain your message; stories that amplify meaning, causing your audience to apply your message; and stories that increase motivation, causing your audience to relate emotionally and take action.

THE BALANCE

Engagement hangs on a delicate balance between credibility and relatability. Influencers need to understand this balance, and work to be equal parts credible and relatable.

- If your audience doesn't see you as credible, they won't care.

- If your audience doesn't see you as relatable, they won't respond.

I know I've missed the mark on this balance many times. As a young entrepreneur I sat in front of many people who seemed to like me and enjoyed having me around but they would never follow my vision or buy my products. I had to face reality that even though they could relate to me, I wasn't very credible in their eyes and so my vision didn't carry any weight.

The interesting thing was once I overcame that and started to have success I began to get the opposite reaction. I had people who would listen to my presentation and say, "no wonder you are successful," or "I know you are going to do great things, I just can't see myself doing it."

I had become credible and lost relatability.
It's really a balance. You need to be relatable so that you

connect, but at the same time sufficiently credible so that your message carries clout.

Credibility is something you build through who you are, what you know, what you do, and how you communicate. Investing in your character, increasing your competency, and improving your communication will build credibility in the eyes of your audience. Credibility is something you have to earn by becoming someone worth listening to.

Relatability comes by being real and approachable. Learning to speak in a conversational tone and not a condescending manner will raise your relatability. No one wants you to talk at them, they want you to talk with them. The word communication comes from the Latin word Communicare, which means common. A great communicator establishes common ground with his audience so that a connection is made. Both sides can relate. Remember the goal of communication is not perfection, but rather connection.

Expert Example

One of the best examples of this balance comes from the movie "The Pursuit of Happyness." The movie is the true story of Chris Gardner (played by Will Smith), a struggling salesman who takes custody of his son as he's beginning a life-changing professional endeavor.

My favorite scene in the movie is the interview Chris has with the board at Dean Witter as he seeks a position in their highly competitive training program that would give him a chance to become a stockbroker. The night before the interview, he is painting his apartment when there is a knock at the door. It turns out to be a policeman who arrests Chris for failure to pay parking tickets and he spends the night in jail. He is released the next morning and runs straight to the interview, disheveled, covered in paint and only wearing a tank top shirt.

You can almost feel the tension as he enters the room. The board members in their finely pressed suits look at him with disdain. Chris addresses the elephant in the room up front by honestly saying, "I've been sitting out there for the last half hour trying to come up with a story that would explain my being here, dressed like this. And I wanted to come up with a story that would demonstrate qualities that I'm sure you all admire here like earnestness, diligence, team playing or something. And I couldn't come up with anything. So the truth is, I was arrested for failure to pay parking tickets and I ran here from the police station." His story made them laugh and relax. Chris showed confidence and related his positive qualities through a simple story. He found a balance of credibility and relatability—through a timely, well-told story. They forgot what he looked like and focused on what he had to offer to their firm. He was admitted into the program, which eventually changed his life.

THE SCIENCE OF STORYTELLING

Chapter 3

THE SCIENCE OF
STORYTELLING

"Stories are how we think. They are how we make meaning of life. Call them schemes, scripts, cognitive maps, mental models, metaphors, or narratives. Stories are how we explain how things work, how we make decisions, how we justify our decisions, how we persuade others, how we understand our place in the world, create our identities, and define and teach social values."

– Dr. Pamela Rutledge

We are genetically programmed to learn through stories. It's who we are. It's how we function. Storytelling was the first form of communication historically and is the first form of communication that we encounter as children. As human beings we crave stories. We love to hear stories and we love to share stories. We learn and retain stories before we can read. Our minds intuitively understand story structure and process the message, information and detail contained therein. But stories are more than that. Stories are our universal storehouse of knowledge, beliefs, values, attitudes, passions, dreams, imagination, and vision.

It is an ancient need to be told stories. And the most memorable stories, those that best meet that inherent desire in us all, come with a great storyteller. That is what this book is about. Helping you to tell a great story so that those who hear it will be influenced greatly by your message.

THE SCIENCE LESSON

When I speak on storytelling to audiences, I will inevitably have an intellectual who will ask me to explain how what I am teaching works scientifically. They ask, "Why are stories influential? What do they do to our brain?" If you are one of those intellectuals, this section is for you.

In our brains, we have cells that are called mirror neurons.

Mirror neurons are incredible. They allow us as human beings to be able to experience, feel, and understand other people's intentions, actions, and emotions. That may sound far-fetched, but scientific research has definitively shown that this is how we can feel empathy and intuition with other people.

Have you ever felt that connection with others? Have you ever had someone who fully understood you? They will make a comment or ask you a question and you think, "Wow, you do understand what I'm feeling!" That empathy comes because of the mirror neurons they have activated in their brain. They have the ability to feel and experience what you're feeling because of a very real, very human, scientific process.

As a storyteller, if we learn how to really tell a story we can activate the mirror neurons of our listeners so that they begin to experience the story as if it were their own. Why is this important? Because if they experience it, then the ah-ha moment, solution or conclusion to the story will become theirs. They will own it. They will absorb it and adopt it, and when they do, they become much more compliant and interested in you and in your objectives. You will have their full and undivided attention. That's where influence really starts to come into play.

Imagine that the story you're using to sell your product tells about a positive experience one of your clients had while using the product. By sharing the story in a relatable and compelling manner you will activate the mirror neurons of your prospects; they will begin to feel the positive experience of your client, and in turn see how your product can become the solution to their needs as well.

The same applies to a strategy that you're sharing, or a vision that you're presenting for your people, or to any information that you may be teaching. If you can activate the mirror neurons of your audience through effective storytelling, your listeners will put themselves in the story and experience it as if it were their own.

That is the science of storytelling that makes it influential.

SEVEN REASONS STORIES WORK

Stories are effective vehicles to teach, to inspire, to inform, and to educate, for one crucial, all-important reason: they work.

Executive coach Paul Heagan identifies seven reasons why stories are able to engage, connect, and compel, and cause the listener to pay attention, process, absorb, and remember.

The seven reasons are:

1. **Stories are a common ground.** We all have a story to tell (whether we are accustomed to articulating it or not). When we share a story, we are inviting someone else to do the same. While some stories may seem to be more profound or gripping than others, as humans we respect that each person's story matters to them as much as ours does to us. Stories put us on the same level and help us realize our common struggles, dreams, joys, and fears.

2. **Stories ignite the imagination and senses, not just the brain.** Communicating well is not only an intellectual exercise; to really connect with people we need to bring them into our experience. Stories do that. When you paint a picture with your words, people put themselves in that picture.

3. **Stories are a safe way to reveal our priorities and sense of self.** The stories you choose to tell—whether they are about your parents, your grandparents, your children, a good friend, an adventure or experience—say a lot about what matters to you. People can hear your emotion, the conviction in your voice, the quiet pain or joy you express, and invariably come away with a deeper appreciation of what has shaped you and made you the person you are.

4. **Stories are simply more effective and durable in conveying information and truth.** We all have mental photos stored in our brains from our own experience. When someone tells a story, we retrieve those images and link them together to form our own mental image. I have observed time and time again that people absorb information better and retain it longer when

they can form and then recall that mental picture. People will forget fairly quickly how some information made them think, but will long remember how a story made them feel.

5. **Stories are viral.** If you as a leader are hoping to expand your influence in your organization or in your circles, there is no better way to network than with stories. Stories are easy to remember and repeat. The good ones get repeated a lot. The fact is, most of us don't walk around with PowerPoint presentations. What we do walk around with are stories. Tell yours well, and others can and will repeat it for you and be your "voice" in ways you never could be on your own.

6. **Stories stimulate a response and action.**
   The thinking process serves the role of sorting and weighing information, experiences and consequences, but what propels all that thinking into action is how we feel. This is why we have pep rallies and political conventions. It is emotion that launches causes and crusades.

7. **Stories reveal purpose.** We all want to believe we are on The Hero's Journey, the monomyth of novelist

James Joyce—to venture out in life, face struggles, experience victory, and bring it all back to the village of our lives as wiser souls is the stuff of the human condition. Whether you know it or not, your story of your own struggles and your own victories—however modest they may seem to you—has tremendous power to inspire and motivate others and propel them to greater heights.

FIVE PLACES TO USE STORIES

Chapter 4

FIVE PLACES TO
USE STORIES

> "The best leaders ... almost without exception and at
> every level, are master users of stories and symbols."
> – Tom Peters

Have you ever been to a networking group? You know,
the kind where you watch people stand up and give a
30-second, three-minute or five-minute elevator speech
about what they do? My question is, who is most
compelling in these presentations? I went to a networking
meeting recently and it was amazing how simply telling
a story made certain presenters stand out. They were
more credible, more engaging, more relatable, and more
memorable.

The same thing happens at a wedding. When people are

toasting the bride and groom, what engages the wedding party, creates laughter, and brings tears to everyone in attendance? It is not typically the advice that is given that is moving and memorable, it is the stories that are told.

Are stories crucial to every presentation? I believe they are. Stories make you, your products, and your ideas multidimensional. They are captivating and compelling. Every presenter needs to learn the importance of stories as well as the art of storytelling. Stephen Covey learned this lesson from his wife. In his book, Living The Seven Habits, he shares this insight: "For more than forty years, my wife, Sandra, has heard hundreds of my presentations, and almost inevitably, in giving me feedback, she counsels me to use more stories, to give more examples that illustrate the principles and theories I am teaching. She simply says to me, 'don't be so heavy. Use stories people can relate to.' She has always had an intuitive sense for these things and, fortunately, has had absolutely no hesitation to express it! Experience has taught me that Sandra was right and I was wrong. I've come to realize not only that a picture is worth a thousand words, as the Far Eastern expression goes, but that a picture created in the heart and mind of a person by a story is worth ten thousand."

KNOW YOUR AUDIENCE

Great storytellers focus on the audience. They have done their homework, they know who they are speaking to, and they pay close attention to how the audience is responding, whether through their words, their laughter, or through their eyes and body language.

Only when you truly know your audience can you make your message about them. That is what creates influence, and the most important facet of making it about them is to tie your message into their primary motivations. If you find out what drives them, what their hot button is, and make your message align with that drive, you are golden.

Researchers have identified four primary categories that motivate people. I call them the four P's: Pleasure, Prestige, Payoff, Productivity. As we examine them, it's easy to see how each has universal appeal.

Pleasure – People naturally seek enjoyment. They want to be happy. They want their life to be fun and pleasurable. Is the benefit you're presenting to them going to provide it? If so, people will be driven to buy your product, follow your strategy, or subscribe to your ideas.

Prestige – Status and power are tremendously appealing. Show people that they will be viewed as more credible, looked up to, seen as leaders, and they will respond readily to your message.

Payoff – This is the money motivator. When what you are presenting offers the potential to affect a person's bottom line—it will make them rich!—you will definitely have their attention.

Productivity – When you show people how they can accomplish more in less time, with increased output, you not only open the door to a more attractive, less-stressful lifestyle but to myriad ways for them to increase their pleasure, prestige and payoff.

Take care to tailor your stories so they appeal to the four primary motivations and watch what happens. You will see your audience engage and respond at a whole new level.

PUT STORIES TO USE

When you break down communication, there are really only five places where you can use a story. Whether you are talking to friends, teaching a child, instructing a coworker, selling a product, or giving a speech, stories will always be used in one of the following five ways:

- Opening
- Closing
- To Introduce A Point
- To Validate A Point
- To Handle Objections

Each of these story vehicles has a unique and effective role.

1. **Opening** – A story is a great way to start any presentation or conversation. You will automatically set your listeners at ease and instantly engage them. When it comes to presenting, we need to get rid of the pleasantries and jump right into the content. A story is an effective way to do just that. No one wants to hear, "Thank you for having me today," "I'm so glad

to be here," or "It's great to be with you." Instead, draw the audience into a story from the beginning. I start most of my keynotes with a story about Howard Schultz, the innovative CEO of Starbucks. Howard is constantly reminding his team, "We are not in the coffee business serving people; we are in the people business serving coffee." From the beginning of my speech, I want my audience to recognize the commonality we all share—we are all in the people business.

To see a clip of me opening with the Howard Shultz Story, use the link. – bit.ly/ZCLX2o

2. **Conclusion** – If you want to leave your audience on an emotional high, full of hope and inspiration, nothing beats a great story. A story is an excellent way to tie the presentation together and reiterate the main message. When you close with a story it should be something memorable and emotionally charging. It could be a funny story, or a dramatic story, but it needs to move and inspire the audience, as it will be the last thing they will remember.

I love closing my speeches with a powerful story. One

of my favorites is about Michael Downing, a young man who lost the use of all four of his limbs. He was asked to speak to a group of wounded soldiers at the end of World War II. He started out by telling them, "I want you to know that anything is possible, you have a bright future ahead of you and the potential to achieve anything that you desire." The soldiers immediately started booing him. Who was this upstart telling them they could be and do anything they wanted, when they were injured and impaired? Then Michael proceeded to remove a prosthetic right leg, then a prosthetic left leg, then a prosthetic right arm, then a prosthetic left hand. At fourteen he fell off a wagon in a snowstorm, suffered severe frostbite and doctors had to amputate both legs, an arm and a hand at the wrist. Sitting there a stump of a man, he started his speech over: "I want you to know that anything is possible, you have a bright future ahead of you and the potential to achieve anything that you desire."

To see a clip of this inspirational story, use the link – bit.ly/14b3Rhc

3. **To Introduce a Point** – If the audience remembers the story, they will remember the point it made. We all remember morals of stories that are shared. For instance, you have the tortoise and the hare—the moral is slow and steady wins the race. The right story can set up a lesson, share a discovered solution, or introduce a product. It's the story that creates the curiosity, establishes the need and then delivers the point with major impact. When I speak to influencers, one of the key messages I share is to focus on being interested, not interesting. I introduce the idea with the story of my friend's struggle to connect, make friends, and date as she started college. I urged her to focus on being interested, rather than interesting, which made all the difference.

   To view a clip of this story that introduces a point, use the link - bit.ly/ZgB8Qk

4. **To Validate A Point** – Many times a story will be used to support the idea, product or concept that is being discussed. If an idea is presented, a story can validate the application of that idea and make it real. Historically, points are validated using empirical

evidence, facts, figures, and statistics. But hard evidence can be enhanced and brought to life with an effective story. I love what Randy Gage said, "Don't present through facts, figures and other statistics. At least not if you want people to engage and take action. Present through stories. And remember that EMOTION is what causes people to act. Sometimes statistics, data, and scientific evidence is important. But ask yourself how that plays out in the lives of your prospects and find where the emotion is."

> **Expert Tip:** Some people use statistics like a drunken man uses a lamppost—for support rather than illumination. Wrap facts within your stories and they will add to the credibility of the story, be understood in context, and be remembered.

Facts and figures are an important piece of many presentations. But stories need to be an integral part as well. Stories are a great validation to what is being presented; be it a product, idea, lesson, or vision.

My brother and I built a very successful business in direct sales. One of our products is a home spa device whose target market is women who are over 30 years old. Every time I present that product to a prospect, I use my mom's story to validate its effectiveness. The story is relatable—because my mom is a middle-aged woman—and it shows that the product provides the desired results. I am able to tie facts and figures relating to the product into the story. To see me share my mom's story – click on the link - bit.ly/14b4ebP

5. **To Handle Objections** – One of the most common methods to overcome objections of a listener can be summed up in these three words: Feel. Felt. Found. The idea is to relate to the objections of your listeners and gently move them toward a new way of thinking. A response might go like this, "Tom, I understand how you **feel.** In fact, I **felt** the same way, but the more I researched it, I **found** that it just made sense." Then follow that with the story of your own experience. There is no better way to communicate Feel, Felt, Found than through a personal story.

SECTION TWO: SKILLSET

> "Take advantage of every opportunity to practice your communication skills so that when important occasions arise, you will have the gift, the style, the sharpness, the clarity, and the emotions to affect other people."
> – Jim Rohn

The skillset of storytelling is both the science and the art. It is the structure and the delivery.

In this section I will show you how you can find your voice and perfect your craft. We will learn the nitty-gritty of storytelling. This is where we roll up our sleeves and study the three-step formula to craft a compelling story. We will learn the hook of an influential story as well as time-proven techniques that bring the audience into your story.

As with any worthwhile pursuit—whether it's studying the piano or violin, pursuing a career on Broadway, chasing the dream of competing in the Olympics—it also takes practice, practice, practice to become an adept storyteller.

Behind every spellbinding storyteller who makes it look as easy and effortless as falling out of bed is a great deal of dedication to developing the absolutely essential skills that make it appear that simple.

This is where we move from the conceptual to the practical.

SKILLSET: CHAPTER FIVE

THE FOUNDATION

Chapter 5

THE FOUNDATION

> "I realized the importance of having a story today is what really separates companies. People don't just wear our shoes, they tell our story."
>
> – Blake Mycoskie, CEO, Tom's Shoes

The largest franchise business in the world is Subway. With over 35,000 locations, Subway surpassed McDonald's in 2010 and continues to grow. So what is their secret? According to Entrepreneur.com, the #1 reason for Subway's success is telling a great story. Subway found a compelling story in Jared Fogle, its spokesman who weighed 425 pounds as a college freshman. Now Fogle is running marathons. It is his before and after—and after—tale that cemented the chain in the American mindset as a healthier alternative to other fast-food restaurants.

The right story can be a gold mine. Story creates a spark that ignites a new awareness. It is such an influential tool that if you use it constructively, it can change people's hearts and minds. That is why Janet Litherland said, "Stories have power. They delight, enchant, touch, teach, recall, inspire, motivate, challenge. They help us understand. They imprint a picture on our minds. Consequently, stories often pack more punch than sermons. Want to make a point or raise an issue? Tell a story."

Our lives revolve around stories. The stories we tell ourselves, the stories we tell others and the stories others tell us. Facebook, the largest social media platform in the world, recently changed the word "status updates" to the word "stories." When you hear about others, you read their story. When you share with others, you share your story. Stories are life's currency. We are constantly exchanging stories, but those who learn to tell stories well have a unique ability to teach, to persuade, to motivate, and to move people.

"Stories are the creative conversion of life itself into a more powerful, clearer, more meaningful experience. They are the currency of human contact."
– Robert McKee

THE DEFINITION

In order for us to tell influential stories, we need to define or quantify what makes up an influential story. The definition that I like best comes from Annette Simmons in *Whoever Tells The Best Story Wins.*

"Story is a reimagined experience narrated with enough detail and feeling to cause your listeners' imaginations to experience it as real."

So how do we do that? How do we tell a story in a way that causes the listener to experience it as if it is real?

When you master the art of storytelling, you learn to make your story about your audience. You learn to tell your story so that it activates the mirror neurons of the listener causing them to experience it as if it were their own. Why is that amazing? Because if they experience it as real, then the solution, the ah-ha moment, becomes their own.

When you are mastering this art, always remember that the first building block in influential storytelling is that you don't retell a story—you relive a story.

Expert Tip: You Don't Retell A Story—You Relive A Story

BRING THE AUDIENCE INTO YOUR STORY

The number one way to relive a story instead of just retell a story is to bring the audience into the story.

There are three ways to do this:
1. Place Them In The Scene
2. Create Curiosity
3. Reinforce relatability

The first way to bring the audience into the story is to physically place them in the scene. If you were to retell a story, you may start by saying, "I was standing on my back porch one day." But when you relive the story, you place the audience in the scene by saying, "If you had been standing with me on my back porch." Do you see the difference? Here is another example: "Tom, if you had been sitting in my office during the interview, you would have been cracking up." What does that do? That automatically places your listener in the scene and it engages his mirror neurons in a way that he can start to relive the story.

There's a story that I tell when I speak on the two most important days of your life. In the story there's a really emotional, impactful phone call that a friend of mine receives. So when my friend hangs up the phone, I place the audience in the story by saying, "Imagine receiving that phone call, what emotion would you be feeling?" By placing them in the story they are reliving it themselves.

Expert Tip: The word "imagine" is a great word to use in storytelling because it automatically turns on the right side of the listeners' brain and they go directly into the scene where you're putting them.

The second way to bring the audience in is to ask

questions that create curiosity. This is typically done at the beginning of the story. But you can't ask just any question. The question must be a "you" focused question. Remember that as an influencer, your focus is on the audience. If you look on page one of this book, you will see that I started the book with a "you" focused question:

Have you ever met one of your heroes?

Here is the truth. No one cares about your story unless it pertains to them. So when you say, "I want to tell you my story," the audience is thinking, "Why? I don't care about your story." Begin instead with a "you" focused question and step into their world. Then, when you have their engagement, you can bring them into your world with your story.

Let me illustrate. I often do goal-setting seminars. Instead of saying, "I want to tell you my experience with goals," I will use a "you" focused question to open them up. I will say, "What stops you from achieving your goals?" If the response is procrastination, I can say, "Absolutely, I would guess we all have procrastinated at times. I know I have, in fact...." And I have a perfect segue into my story. We have to make it about them by creating curiosity.

The most natural place to create curiosity with a "you" focused question is at the beginning of a story but it can also be done in the middle. Pretend you are telling a story where something happens to one of the characters. If you're at a turning point in the story and the listener doesn't know how the individual has responded yet, a great question to create curiosity would be, "How would you react to that?" Then you would pause, allowing a moment for reflection, and then you would tell them how the character in the story reacted. That creates curiosity and it brings the audience in. To bring the audience into the story, there are times when you need to step out of the story and ask a "you" focused question.

The third way to bring the audience into the story is to reinforce relatability. This is done throughout to continue to bring your story back to the audience. You do this by saying things like, "Do you know what I mean?" "Have you ever felt that before?" "I don't know if this has happened to you." If you bring the audience into the story by creating curiosity, then you want to keep them in the story by reinforcing relatability. It is an effective way to turn your presentation into a conversation, moving it from a monologue to a dialogue.

THE BLUEPRINT

Chapter 6

THE BLUEPRINT

> "We want a story that starts out with an earthquake and works its way up to a climax."
> – Samuel Goldwyn

Would you ever try building a house by simply grabbing some wood, a hammer and nails? Or would you first design the home, create a blueprint, and then approach it with a plan? The answer is obvious and yet when we are communicating with others we seem to just say whatever comes to mind and hope that our message moves people the way that we desire. One of the questions that I get most often is, "Ty, is there a step-by-step process to create an influential story?" The answer is yes! There is an exact blueprint you can use, an actual model to follow, a sequence, if you will. Once you understand that blueprint it becomes incredibly easy to craft the perfect story to connect with your audience, to sell your product, to teach a point or to convey your vision.

THE STARTING POINT

The starting point of any story is the call to action. What is the purpose of your story? What is the outcome you are seeking? What do you want to have happen to the audience because of listening to your story? It could be to present a new idea, introduce a take-away message, sell a product, get a vote, move them to take action, get a laugh, or motivate them. Once you identify the purpose of the story, the call to action becomes the measuring stick against which all of the content of the story is considered.

When it comes to storytelling here is the most important rule: If it's not necessary to say, it's necessary not to say. What does that mean? It means that we need to be succinct and concise. We want to say things in as few words as possible. We want to keep the audience engaged. We want all of the information to lead to the call to action of the story.

Only the pertinent information stays. Throw the rest out.

If there is entertainment value to it; if it helps to create curiosity; if it brings the audience in; if it adds to the relatability or the credibility of the story, then obviously keep it in. And we determine that by judging it against the call to action. We look at each part and say, "If it adds to it, it stays. If it takes away, take it out."

Being able to communicate concisely is paramount to making sure your message is heard. One of my favorite comedians is Jerry Seinfeld. Jerry is a great communicator and he taught a great lesson on communication when he said, "I will spend an hour taking an eight word sentence and editing it down to five."

In comedy, the fewer the words between the set-up and the punch word, the bigger the laugh. In business communications, change the punch word or phrase to impact phrase. The lesson is still the same.

In our high-paced, content-filled world, if we want our communication to be heard and understood, we need to be succinct. You have probably listened to people who tell a two-minute story in seven minutes. That's not what we're looking for. We would rather tell a seven-minute story in two minutes and provide more impact and therefore have more influence.

THE SEQUENCE

Every story is three parts: a beginning, middle, and an end.

For influential stories the sequence is:
- The Setup
- The Struggle
- The Solution

The setup is the opening of a story, where you provide the details needed for the story to make sense. The setup does three things, and it does them quickly:

1. Provides context
2. Sets the scene
3. Introduces the characters

You do those three things as quickly as possible. One of the critical mistakes that people make is taking too long in the setup. If you ramble on and on, you will do more than distract your audience. You will drive them away. Keep it short and purposeful.

The key to making your story work is to introduce your characters and then throw your characters into a struggle. This is the point that most influencers don't realize. It's the struggle that is the hook for the story. There is something about confrontation and conflict that grabs our attention. It engages emotion and draws us in. The best examples of this are children's stories. Every famous child's story has a struggle that has to be overcome. It is so obvious that the other night as I told my kids a bedtime story, my four-year-old son said, "Dad, there has to be something bad that happens in the story or else it isn't a good story."

Now what do I mean by struggle? If you think back to your elementary school days, there are five types of struggle:

- Man vs. man
- Man vs. Nature
- Man vs. Society
- Man vs. Environment
- Man vs. Himself

Think about it. These five categories of conflict are responsible for virtually every movie plot ever filmed.

For a man vs. man struggle, think of the movie "Rocky." You have two boxers literally fighting against each other in the ring. The drama of the man vs. man struggle is the hook for the story.

For man vs. nature, think of the movie, "Twister." The conflict for the tornado chasers comes when the tornado chases them. Maybe you have a story about being stuck in a snowstorm or a hurricane; when you share your story you will see that it is the struggle that draws people in.

One of the best examples of man vs. society is the movie "Braveheart." William Wallace, played by Mel Gibson, is a commoner fighting to change a nation. The story, especially the struggle, is riveting.

There are a lot of examples of man vs. environment struggles. Maybe you are in a negative situation at work, or even with your family. A great movie example comes from "The Pursuit of Happyness," which I referenced in Chapter Two. In the movie, Chris Gardner is fighting his environment to break out of poverty.

Some of the best stories ever told are man vs. himself struggles. Such conflicts are common to us all. And when we are real with our personal struggles, we become relatable. Think of the movie "Castaway," starring Tom

Hanks. It is about a man deserted on an island who has to deal with the mental conflict, loneliness, and anxiety of the situation, and it is a classic.

Whatever the conflict, it is the blueprint for successful storytelling because you hook the audience with the struggle and then you help them with the solution.

Imagine going to a movie. The previews of this movie have hyped it for months. You are excited. You sit down with a big drink in one hand and large popcorn in the other hand. The movie starts, and it is about a man who merrily skips his way through life. Everything he tries works out. He never experiences any trials or feels any pain. There are no ups or downs. No struggles. Wouldn't you walk out of the movie and say, "Who cares!" Without a struggle, there is nothing engaging about the story.

Think about the movie "Titanic." The movie has the setup, where context is provided, the scene is set and characters are introduced. As soon as they hit the iceberg and the water starts coming in—boom—they are thrown into a struggle and you are on the edge of your seat. You automatically start thinking, "What are they going to do?" "How will they get everyone off the ship?" "Are they going to die?"

Now here is another lesson from Titanic. Imagine if the water level stopped at their ankles. That would be pretty anticlimactic, wouldn't it? So what do we learn from "Titanic?" We learn that a great storyteller introduces the struggle and then incrementally increases it. Think of it as raising the water level. It rises from the ankles to the waist and then the shoulders, creating more and more drama. When the struggle reaches its peak, you have a climax and it is at the climax that the solution is provided.

The solution to overcome the struggle may be an idea, a strategy or a product, and whoever or whatever provides the solution becomes the hero of the story. For example: if your story is about a client who had an issue with time management and your product was the solution, then the product is the hero. If your goal is to sell time management products, you have achieved your objective. Depending on the story being told, you may be the hero, or it could be a mentor, or a book, or a product, or a stranger. Remember that if your struggle is relatable to the audience, then the solution will be credible and the hero will gain credibility.

So how do we make the struggle relatable? If your focus is on the audience and you know your audience, then you want to make the struggle in your story match the pain in your audience's life. What do I mean by that? The struggle has to be relatable to the audience, because if the struggle is relatable, then the solution will be credible. If you know your audience is dealing with lack of follow-through, for example, and you can share your own struggle with the same issue in a relatable way, then the solution that you discovered will become their solution as well. Your story becomes their story; your solution becomes their solution. That is why Elizabeth Lyon observed, "The universality of human suffering and struggle compels your reader (or listener)—a stranger—to invest in your story." Once you hook them with the struggle, you are in a position to help them with the solution.

Let me share one last thought with you on the blueprint. I have observed that most of the time when influencers are telling their own stories, they try to come from a position of power and make themselves look good. They are unwilling to talk about their own struggles. The problem this creates is a lack of relatability. If you will be real and share your struggles, you will be relatable. You can do this and still be credible, because don't forget the model. The model is struggle-to-solution, which means that you are not sharing your struggles to say that everything is horrible. You are sharing reality, which is relatable, and then providing a credible solution.

If you will adopt this model of struggle-to-solution for all of your stories, including your own, you will find that your influence will increase and your message will have the impact you intend.

EXPERT EXAMPLE

Let me illustrate. I have become known for a story that I tell, called the 4C Story. It is a funny experience that happened to me while traveling that has a great takeaway message. You can read it below and watch the live version, but pay attention to the setup, the struggle and the solution. It is a man vs. man struggle that I introduce early and incrementally increase. The struggle is relatable and the solution is credible. It is a step-by-step illustration of the blueprint we have just discussed, and audiences around the world love it!

THE 4C STORY

You can read the 4C story below or to view a video clip of the 4C story – use this link: bit.ly/13gXv0J

Flying out of Salt Lake City, I almost always fly Delta. Because I fly with Delta so often, I am upgraded to first class virtually every time I fly. Not too long ago I was going to Oakland, California—a quick, painless flight—and I was upgraded to first class. I was the first one on the plane. I sat down in seat 4B, pulled out my iPad and was getting a few things done before takeoff.

As I was sitting there, looking down, all of a sudden a guy says, "You are in my seat. Get up." He said it just like that: "Get up!"

I looked up and said, "Wow, I'm sorry, what seat are you in?"

He said, "Do you realize this is first class? I'm sitting in first class and this is my seat." (Don't you love dealing with difficult people?) I said, "I know, I am in first class also— what is your seat?" Then he asked what I still view as the dumbest question I've ever been asked, "Did you pay to sit in first class or just get upgraded, because I paid for my seat."

I replied, "Well that stinks. I was upgraded, which means I paid a lot less money for the exact same seat.   What seat is yours?" "4C," he answered. And I thought, you have got to be kidding me, your seat is right across the aisle.

"Then that is your seat over there," I said, and pointed to the other side of the aisle.

He simply turned and sat down in his seat, with no apology whatsoever. By then I couldn't help myself, so I said, "You know what, you would suck at what I do." He said, "Why is that?" And I said, "Because you are not good with people. In fact you are horrible with people. Just be nice. It's not that hard."

THE DELIVERY

Chapter 7

THE DELIVERY

| "Don't learn the tricks of the trade—learn the trade."
| – James Bennis

Two common questions I'm asked are, "Where do stories come from?" and "Where do you find stories?" My answer to both is the same: it all starts with awareness. There are many great sources for stories, and great storytellers are carefully and constantly observing life to gather them.

Stories can come from history, books, movies, current events, you name it, but by far the most consistent and reliable source is your own experience. That is the mother lode. The most powerful stories are your own.

This should become a habit for you. Always be on the lookout for story material in your day-to-day life. Things happen all the time, little experiences that provide the compelling fabric for your stories. Maybe you're watching a movie and you think, "Wow, that's a perfect teaching moment, that's a great story that I can share." Maybe you're reading a book and you can pull a story out of it. Perhaps you're watching the news and there's a story there. Pay close attention to the experiences that happen to you. They provide the building blocks for your stories.

The most powerful stories are personal. The more personal, the more powerful. It's natural to say, "I don't have any personal stories," or "My story isn't special." We usually don't view ourselves or our life as very interesting. But the truth is, we all have stories to tell, and they are interesting and compelling. If we'll step back and look at the experiences that we've had, the struggles, the triumphs, the ups and the downs, we will discover amazing stories that each of us has to tell.

THE TWO TYPES OF PERSONAL STORIES

Personal stories come in two types: Experienced and Observed.

Experienced stories are the ones that happen directly to us. I shared my story earlier of the struggle that I had, and the things I needed to learn, before I was able to build a successful business with my brother. That's a personal experience that became a story. Such stories are full of the interactions, the personal struggles, the trials and triumphs, and hilarious experiences of our lives.

Observed experiences are stories that we witness and then relate. We may have just seen an accident but not been personally involved. Or we've watched an incredible struggle-to-solution story of someone close to us. These are other people's stories but observing them allows us to identify the details and values in them and in turn share them with others.

The key is to personalize these observed experiences so they become relevant to you and to your audience. Let me give you an example:

If you were to tell a story about Abraham Lincoln, obviously that's not going to be a personal story, but you can personalize it by simply saying, "I don't know if you've ever studied much about Abraham Lincoln but he's one of my heroes."

Great storytellers personalize every story. Personalizing is what gives a story power and allows the audience to make a connection and relate.

But a word of caution: be careful in using other people's stories too often. As effective as observed stories can be, when you share your own experiences you make yourself real and relatable and build credibility. People want to know that you know and have lived what you are talking about and are not just sharing from a book or someone else's experiences. There is great value in that.

PERFECT YOUR CRAFT

Theory raises people's hopes, but practice raises their income.

In the first two chapters of the Skillset section, we examined the structure of storytelling. You now understand the three-step formula for an influential story. You know how to relive a story and bring your audience in. You know how to use the struggle as the hook and the solution as the help. I have taught you how to craft a great story.

What I can't teach you is how to deliver your story. Sure, I will give you tips and in the next section I will give you tools, but the art, the delivery, your voice—that only comes as all worthwhile things come. Through practice.

The structure is science based, but the art is individual. Through trial and error and repetition, and more repetition, is how you will find your voice and perfect your craft. And I promise that you will.

I had an interesting experience when I was 19 years old. I served a two-year mission for my church. While I was on my mission, I was out teaching people everyday. I was in Portugal, so I learned a new language and I had to learn how to communicate in that language, which was a feat in and of itself. But the entire time I was there, I had a companion. My companion changed from time to time but we were always in twos. And one of the things that we did, every day, literally every single day for two years, is we would have a one-hour companionship study in the morning. In that companionship study we would sit down for the first 15 minutes and review teaching concepts and discuss ideas of how to share our message, and then for the next 45 minutes we would role-play that message. If you have ever role-played you know how awkward it can be. I can tell you, for two 19-year-old boys, it was awkward. In the beginning we were embarrassed doing it and there was no one around to be embarrassed in front of. It just felt weird and uncomfortable. Yet we kept doing it day in and day out. After a little practice, it became less awkward and slowly but surely it became pretty natural. And after doing it every day for two years, role-playing became second nature.

Role-playing has helped me become a great storyteller as well. It is a habit that I want you to adopt. You need to learn how to tell your stories, and as obvious as this may sound, the only way to do it is to tell your stories. Role-play to yourself at first if that is the most comfortable, but then step out and get feedback from others. It could be from a family member, friend, or colleague. It could be someone on your team, a fellow teacher, or your sales manager. It doesn't matter who it is, just that you do it. Solicit feedback and practice, practice, practice.

Once you are in the habit of role-playing, I want you to take it a step farther and record yourself. Audio is great, but video is better. The first time you listen and watch yourself live it is shocking! I believe we are our harshest critics but you can't critique what you don't see or hear.

When you record yourself and analyze it, you will really be able to take your storytelling to the next level.

Here are some great ways to analyze a recording:

- As you listen, ask yourself "Would I buy from me? Am I persuasive and compelling?"
- Is the story engaging?
- Listen for filler words such as "um" and "you know" and eliminate them.
- Does it feel like a presentation or a conversation?
- Are you balancing credibility and relatability?
- Are you bringing the audience in so they can relive the story?
- Does your story have a setup, struggle, and solution?
- Do you get to the struggle fast enough and escalate the struggle in an engaging and emotional way?
- Is your call to action strong?

Additional ideas for video:

- If it is live, watch for audience reaction and take note of where you get engagement and why.
- Watch the video in fast forward and see if you are nervously pacing back and forth across the stage

instead of standing and striding confidently.

- Watch the video on mute and pay close attention to facial expressions, gesture, posture, and movement (is your body language helping or hurting the story?).

Some of my greatest growth as a young entrepreneur and storyteller came when I began recording every phone call and every appointment. As I listened and learned what worked, what didn't work, and what I could improve on, I went back to my role-playing and made changes. Then I would record the next meeting and as I improved, so did my results.

As a speaker, I have learned more about what works, what doesn't work, and where I need improvement by watching video of me on stage that any other way. I do it constantly—because perfecting a craft is a life-long pursuit.

TELL IT LIKE IT'S THE FIRST TIME

Should you memorize your story or should you just give it off the cuff? I've heard experts argue both ways. The spontaneous storyteller would contend that a memorized story is canned, inauthentic and less engaging, while a practiced storyteller would say that you can perfect the story and deliver it best when you put in the work beforehand.

I believe that you should memorize a story to the point that it becomes so natural for you to say that it seems as though you're telling it for the first time. Great storytellers tell a story, even if they've told it a million times, like it's their inaugural delivery. They develop a style that is natural, organic, and conversational so that people will engage and it feels authentic.

And remember, this is the audience's first time hearing it; to them it needs to sound like it's your first time telling it.

Expert Tip: Spontaneity is on the far side of preparation

I'll give you a good example: I've had a chance to share the stage on numerous occasions with Olympic gold medalist Peter Vidmar. Peter Vidmar is in the speaker's hall of fame. He's an amazing speaker. His story is incredible because he shares the experience that he had in the 1984 Olympic Games where he not only won an individual gold medal in pommel horse, he was also part of the gold medal-winning US men's gymnastics team.

I know that Peter's story is memorized because I have heard him tell it enough times that I think I have it memorized too. Every time, Peter tells the same story. His pauses are identical, he laughs at the same parts, and he says things the same way. All of it is the same, but you would never know it. I've watched audiences for years and the reaction never changes. They hear the story and they are so engaged because he's such a great storyteller. He tells it with an excitement and an enthusiasm and with the tools and skills that we've been talking about so that his audience is reliving the story with him. He brings them right into it, he engages them, he balances credibility and relatability. He makes it funny and interesting and relevant. Every single time he speaks he returns, along with the audience, to those Olympic Games in Los Angeles, and has everyone on the edge of their chairs, wondering if he will win gold.

To perfect the art of storytelling, you have to find your voice. You have to learn your stories so well that you can tell them naturally and with great authenticity. You can do that by learning how to role-play. It's going to be awkward at first. I know, I've been through it. But it's just like any other skill, what is once uncomfortable becomes comfortable, even second nature, if you just keep doing it. You have to push through that pain and make it so what you're practicing becomes a natural skillset. Then record and videotape yourself. Go back and listen to the presentation, listen to the interaction, and ask yourself, "Was I engaging?" "Was it interesting?" "Did I bring emotion into it?" "Would I buy from me?" All of those questions will give you insight into what your audience is experiencing, thinking and feeling.

Here's the truth—storytelling, just like communication in any of its forms, is an art that you can perfect if you put enough practice into it. That's what I meant in Chapter 1 when I said climb in the wheelbarrow. It is time to take the science that you have learned and apply it as you work to perfect the personal art of storytelling.

SECTION THREE: TOOLSET

> "Stories are the single most powerful tool in a leader's toolkit"
> – Howard Gardner, *Harvard University psychologist*

When you have a repair project around the house and you reach for your toolbox, you have different tools at your fingertips. Some jobs may require a hammer, while others may require a hammer, screwdriver and a saw. It's the job at hand that determines the tools you're going to use.

That is also the way the toolbox works for your stories. There are six tools in the storyteller's toolbox and you may not use all of them for every story, but they are there when you need them.

In this section we will identify and explain how each of these six tools can be used to best effect. They include:

- The two C's That Make Stories Compelling: Curiosity & Characters

- The two D's That Make Stories Dynamic: Dialogue & Details
- The two M's That Make Stories Memorable: Movement & Metaphors

These are the tools that make your stories come alive, that turn them multi-dimensional and render them compelling, dynamic and memorable. Used deftly and correctly, they will take your storytelling to the next level.

THE TWO C'S THAT MAKE STORIES COMPELLING

Chapter 8

THE TWO C'S THAT MAKE STORIES COMPELLING

> "Storytelling is by far the most underrated skill in business."
> – Gary Vaynerchuck

CURIOSITY

We want our stories to be compelling. We want the audience to dive in, feel the struggle, experience the emotion, relate to the characters, and engage so that when the solution is provided, it will be acted upon. That is the essence of an influential story and it starts by creating curiosity.

In Chapter Five, we discussed "you" focused questions that generate curiosity and bring the audience into your stories. As an influencer, if your focus is on your audience, then you need to look at the story from the audience's perspective. When you put yourself in the position of your listeners, you will be able to know what they are thinking, and if you know what they are thinking, you will dramatically increase the power that you have to influence them. With this understanding you can use curiosity to enhance the stories that you tell.

QUESTIONS AND ANSWERS

Every good story engages the audience with curiosity by creating questions in the audience's mind—questions that will be answered by the time the story ends.

For effective influencers, this is the storytelling formula:

- Questions create curiosity, curiosity creates engagement, engagement creates seeking for answers, answers create satisfaction, and satisfaction creates influence.

The equation begins with posing compelling questions that produce audience engagement. Next come the answers—the important tie that binds everything together. The significance of supplying satisfying answers to the questions you've posed cannot be overstated. Fail to satisfactorily answer your questions and you will disengage your audience. Have you ever walked away from a movie and said, "I just didn't get it, what happened?" Or "That didn't seem to wrap up completely." You leave feeling dissatisfied—and you disengage. Tell a story without acceptably answering the questions you've posed and you'll be greeted with a similar reaction. Your audience will disengage, pushed away from your story because you've sent them down a road and haven't brought them back.

Let me give you an example. Let's revisit my mom's story with the galvanic spa that I shared in chapter 4. If you would like to see it again—click on this link: bit.ly/14b4ebP

As the story unfolded you may have asked several questions. First, when I told you she got the galvanic spa treatment: "Did it work?" And when I said she tried it out: "what happened?" Followed by: "What difference did she see?" When I answered those questions as the story continued, you might have then wondered: "What actually happened on her face?" And when she decided to use it for cellulite, your question might have been: "Does it actually work for cellulite? Did she see the same results as the study?"

Can you see how, in telling my mom's story, I'm constantly creating questions and answering them in turn—all while moving in the direction of the call to action? The questions create the curiosity that keeps the audience engaged in the story.

Expert Tip: To understand the questions in your audiences' mind—record your story and listen to it, paying attention to the questions or curiosity that pop into your mind.

The idea of curiosity engaging the audience really became clear to me when I started watching movies with my wife Sarah after we got married. Most of us have an internal dialogue in our minds when we watch a movie. We are always thinking, "I wonder if he did it?" or "What is going to happen next?" When I watch a movie with Sarah, she has an external dialogue. All the questions that come up in a movie—she says them out loud, and directs them at me. At first I thought it was annoying, now I find it kind of cute and endearing. A movie, if it's done well, is a great story and Sarah's external dialogue has helped me to see how the writers and directors create questions and how they answer them. Hearing the questions also accentuates how imperative it is that they get answered. Movies—bad movies—don't satiate the curiosity and leave the audience frustrated. The same can be said of bad stories.

Here are some of the common mistakes that create what I call cliffhanger stories that leave the audience disengaged:

- Introduce a character but don't give enough information, leaving the audience confused how the character is connected to the story.

- Move from one scene or experience to another without wrapping it up and answering open questions.

- Throw in tangents that have no discernable relationship to the main story, creating unrelated and unresolved curiosity.

Remember, effective storytelling gives equal balance to

questions and answers. Author Tamora Pierce put it like this in *The Trickstar's Choice: "Curiosity killed the cat," Fesgao remarked, his dark eyes unreadable. Aly rolled her eyes. Why did everyone say that to her? "People always forget the rest of the saying," she complained. "And satisfaction brought it back."*

TAKING CURIOSITY TO THE NEXT LEVEL

So how do effective storytellers pose the questions that arouse great curiosity in their audience? They do this by the way they say things, by the twists and the turns, by the sequencing, by the way a character responds, and by creating tension and suspense.

Let me give you an example. In Chapter 1, I finished with the story of the Great Blondin. There is a part of the story where The Great Blondin decides to tightrope walk across Niagara Falls. If I would have opened with, "While he was in New York, he decided to tightrope walk across Niagara falls." I would have given it all away and failed to create any curiosity. Instead, I said, "It was in New York that he discovered what would make him famous." That line invites a question and piques curiosity, engaging the listener. The question is, "What did he discover?" Through curiosity, I'm setting the stage for what comes later. He took a rope and stretched it across Niagara Falls ...

Curiosity compels an audience to jump into your story, to claim it as their own. They get hooked because they want the answers to their questions. If you want to captivate your audience then learn to tell stories in a way that creates suspense and surprise. Curiosity is what will keep them intently tuned to your every word.

CHARACTERS

The second 'C' that creates compelling stories is characters. Every good story has interesting characters. Many times your characters are what give the strongest connection to your audience. Do you remember why I use my mom's story to sell the galvanic spa? It is because she is the perfect character; she represents my client.

As you decide which stories to use with which audience, ask yourself: Are the characters relatable to those who are hearing the story? You, as the storyteller, aren't always and don't necessarily have to be relatable to your audience. But your characters do. If your listeners can easily slip into their shoes, feel what they're feeling, imagine experiencing what they're experiencing, then they will vicariously relate to you as the storyteller and influencer.

This idea was proven to me by an experience I had in San Francisco. I gave a speech to about 200 people. I was talking about the galvanic spa and in the speech I shared my mom's story. Afterward a woman in her late 40's approached me and said, "That was just a great speech; you are so relatable." In the back of my mind I thought, "How in the world am I relatable to you? I'm half your age and I'm a man." And then she said, "I loved the story about your mom. I just got my galvanic spa, I can't wait to see if I have the same results." Right then it hit me—she found me relatable because she related to the character in my story.

When I speak to high school students, I share several stories from when I was in high school, which makes me instantly relatable because the character in my story (a younger me) is someone they can connect with. If I were asked to speak at a senior citizens center, I would want to share a story or two about the wisdom my grandparents shared with me. Through my grandparents, my audience could connect with me.

Carefully choosing characters that are relatable to the audience satisfies the first rule of storytelling: you must put the audience first. Everything you do as an influencer has to be about them. The audience's perspective is the only one that matters. In leadership, in sales, in speaking, or in teaching, if you can step back and, instead of asking "How was that delivered?", ask, "How was that received?" you're going to be light years ahead of most people.

Of course, audiences usually don't consist of just one person. They are typically a collection of individuals. And studies have shown that in any given audience you will find three different types of learners. You'll have visual learners, audible learners, and kinesthetic, or hands-on, learners. The acronym is VAK: Visual, Audible, Kinesthetic. And if there are three types of learners, then you need to know how to connect the characters in your story to each type.

To do this, your characters need three things:
First, they need to be seen.

Second, they need to be heard.

Third, they need to be understood.

Seen

Visual learners remember what they see. So it's important to help them view the characters. How do you do that? By right up front giving a brief line of description that creates an image in the mind of the audience. Paint the outline and then let the audience use imagination to fill in the details. Why is that important? Because it mentally engages your listeners, even if it's only on a subconscious level. Let's look again at my mom's spa story. The brief description I gave of my mom was, "She's in her mid-50's and she has used all sorts of products to take care of her skin." For the context of the story, and the purpose of selling that product, that's all you need to know about her. I don't overdo it because I want the audience engaged and they can create the rest of the details in their mind. They may picture her a little bit differently than I picture her, but the point is not that they get it exactly right but that they stay engaged. As long as the important information is there, the rest is up to them. The storyteller creates the image and the audience fills in the rest.

Another way to connect with visual learners is to use visual language throughout the story. When we do a good job of painting a picture or creating an image, our audience members will connect with the story. Later in my mom's story, she describes visually what happened to her face: "It is lifted, feels smoother, and there are less lines and wrinkles." Then my sister visually describes what happened to her legs by saying, "That one has dimples and that one doesn't."

Visual language allows the character to be seen and when the character is seen, it is easier to relate with him or her.

Heard

To come to life and relevance, every character needs to be heard. Most of the stories you hear are shared in the voice of the person telling them. Instead of allowing the character to be heard, they narrate the story, retelling it in their own words and relegating the character to a passive role. Retelling a story through narration puts the audience in the past. Reliving a story, however, through dialogue and imagery, puts the audience in the present. And remember, the foundation for influential storytelling is making it all about them.

Dialogue is so important that we are going to devote the next chapter to it. In this section, though, it is relevant to touch on a couple of key points around using dialogue with characters. If you go back to my mom's story, the conversations, the interaction that she and I had, and that she had with my sister, I don't narrate those, I deliver them in dialogue. I give my mom a chance to be heard, not through me, but through her own voice. Allowing the character to be heard brings the audience into the scene so they are reliving the story and renders the character considerably more relatable because their personality is allowed to emerge. In my mom's story she shares a little bit of a feisty side. She responds to the idea of the galvanic working on cellulite with, "No, that doesn't work." She isn't just easy-going about the whole thing; she has an opinion. Allowing her to be heard in dialogue creates the back and forth that makes the story more interesting and gives it credibility. Again, we'll dive into how to use dialogue really effectively in the next chapter, but first and foremost it is important to recognize the need for our characters to be heard.

Understood

The third thing that a character needs is a chance to be understood.

> **Expert Tip:** "If the audience doesn't know where the character has been, they won't care where they are going." – Craig Valentine

The idea of understanding and relating to the character is part of the struggle-to-solution model. To care about the solution, the audience needs to know that they fit into the struggle and needs to find the struggle relatable.

There are two ways to help your characters be understood:
- By a brief description as they are introduced.
- Through dialogue.

Again, let's use my mom's story as the example.

As I introduce my mom, I say that she has used all sorts of products to take care of her skin. For the purpose of the story, that's enough history. Yes, I could go into how she's used product X and it didn't work; or how she tried product Y and it didn't work. I actually used to do this, and then I found that it took away from the story. It goes back to the rule: If it is not necessary to say, then it becomes necessary not to say.

The brief but succinct history makes my mom relatable and introduces the struggle. Then, later in the story, in dialogue, my Mom tells me more about her history. She tells me that "She has tried everything in the world for cellulite and nothing's worked." Through dialogue she incrementally increases that struggle and provides even more context to her history, making her all the more relatable. We always need to keep in mind the balance of credibility and relatability, because if the audience relates to your characters, then they feel the struggle. And when the struggle becomes more relatable, the ah-ha moment, the solution, the product, the insight, all of that becomes more credible, more actionable, and more influential.

Great stories that create great influence are, in the end, about answers; answers that satisfy and inspire a call to action. To get there, Curiosity and Characters—the Two C's—are absolutely imperative ingredients.

THE TWO D'S THAT MAKE STORIES DYNAMIC

Chapter 9

THE TWO D'S THAT MAKE STORIES DYNAMIC

> "Don't say the old lady screamed—bring her on and let her scream."
> – Mark Twain

DIALOGUE

My favorite tool in the storyteller's toolbox is dialogue. If you can understand how to use this one device, it will take your stories from feeling like a report—which is not engaging—to feeling like an experience—which is. You will see the result in your audiences' eyes, hear it in their laughter, and measure it in the increased results and influence your stories create.

Dialogue makes stories dynamic because it does the

following things:

- Dialogue places the story in the present tense. Remember, the foundation of influential storytelling is that you don't retell a story, you relive a story. It is through dialogue that the experience becomes current, fresh, brand new—something that is unfolding in real time.

- Dialogue does it naturally. You're not saying it, the characters in your story are saying it, inviting the audience into the scene in the process. When you hear something told through dialogue, you picture it, you experience it. It feels much more like a movie than a news report.

- Dialogue adds impact to the important lines. The lines may be funny, and dialogue will make them funnier. The lines may be sharing a strong message, and sharing it in dialogue will make them stronger. Dialogue renders the important messages of your story more vital and impactful by making them stand out.

- Dialogue helps the characters in your story to be relatable. The characters are not just being described, they're being heard, which makes them very real, significant, and relevant to the audience.

BALANCING DIALOGUE & NARRATION

Dialogue is a story's welcome mat. It invites the audience inside, makes them part of the landscape and the emotion. But for all its effectiveness, we can't share a story with nothing but dialogue. A story that relies entirely on dialogue is really not a story, it's theater. And we're not trying to create a theatrical play. In most of the settings in which we're telling a story it wouldn't be appropriate; it would actually be embarrassing and awkward to tell a story in a dramatic, theatrical way.

Somewhere between a report and theater is the perfect story. The art of storytelling is to find just the right mix. The problem is, it isn't a science. There isn't an equation that says your story should be 40 percent narration and 60 percent dialogue. It is an art—and as with any art, the right balance, the right blend, can only be found through practice.

The way to find that balance is to remember that narration

provides context, while dialogue adds impact. Narration is used to set the scene, introduce the characters and tie all the various elements of the story together. Dialogue is used to add impact and power to your stories. If there is a humorous line or an important dramatic line, saying it in dialogue will heighten the effect.

Let me give you an example. If I told a story about my friend John being diagnosed with cancer, I could do it through narration or dialogue.

Narration: My friend John was just diagnosed with cancer.

Dialogue: My friend John just called me and said, "Ty, I have cancer. I don't know what to do …"

Which one is more impactful? More emotional? Which one sounds like a report and which one sounds like an experience?

For an example of dialogue in action, go back and watch the 4C story. As you do, pay attention to the narration and dialogue mix. Note how narration provides context and dialogue adds impact.
- Link - bit.ly/13gXv0J

CIA

There are three different types of dialogue and I use an acronym to help remember them: CIA.

- C stands for Character dialogue,
- I stands for Inner dialogue
- A stands for Audience dialogue

Character dialogue is the most obvious way to add dialogue into our stories. It is the back and forth from one person to another. It allows the characters to deliver their lines themselves, rendering them intimately relatable. Their message thus hits home unfiltered, and with full impact. As Mark Twain advised, "Don't tell me the old lady screamed—bring her on and let her scream." Let your characters deliver their lines and your stories will instantly become more dynamic.

Inner dialogue is a form of dialogue rarely used but it can be very effective. Inner dialogue takes the thought process of the character in the story and gives it a voice. When you use inner dialogue, you're opening up the mind of a character and allowing the audience in, paving the way to greater insight and understanding. Let me give you a couple of examples. I used inner dialogue in the 4C story. When the man said that his seat was 4C, I said, "And I thought, you have got to be kidding me, your seat is right across the aisle." I didn't actually say those words. I only thought them. But in reliving the story, expressing this inner dialogue helps you to see my level of frustration and state of mind. It increases the struggle. It adds perspective. I'm simply taking my inner thought process and giving it a voice.

Another example of inner dialogue can be found in the Howard Schultz story that I shared in Chapter 4. Howard Schultz is the chairman/CEO of Starbucks and I am telling his life story, leading up to the idea that he teaches that we're all in the people business. The story is not about me and it's not in the present tense, so I have to search for areas to find dialogue. I'm able to do that when I'm telling about Howard's visit to Starbucks for the very first time and how he was so impressed he decided then and there he wanted to be part of the company. I honestly don't know if he said it out loud or not but I know that he thought about it and pursued it—so I let him deliver his line in dialogue. I say, "When Howard left Starbucks, he said, 'I am going to be part of that company.'" Allowing Howard's inner dialogue to be expressed adds impact and gives insight into his resolve and determination. It is so much stronger than simply saying in narration, "Howard decided he was going to be a part of the company." Inner dialogue makes the character, and the story, come alive.

Audience dialogue is when you take the thought process of your listeners and turn it into dialogue. If you have your finger on the pulse of an audience, if you understand what they are thinking, then you can bring out their thought process and put it in a dialogue form. One of my favorite stories to tell is the story of Mel Fisher. Mel Fisher is the greatest treasure hunter the world has ever known. I tell his story to teach the concepts of taking action and being persistent in going after your goals. Mel searched the ocean floor for 17 years before he found the treasure of the Atocha, which is the largest shipwreck treasure that's ever been found. I love to share this story to network marketers or people involved in direct sales, and there's a point in the story where I put the audience's thought process into dialogue to reinforce relatability. Network marketers are involved in an unconventional business and pride themselves as people who think differently. So there's a point in the story where I say, "Mel decided to sell his business, to pick up his family, move across the country and search for treasure full time." And I pause for just a minute and I then say, "Now most people would think that's crazy. But all of you are network marketers so you're probably thinking, 'Yeah, that makes a lot of sense.'"

Using the audience's thought process as dialogue almost always gets the biggest laugh, because there's something funny about taking what the audience is thinking in a very relatable way and putting it into verbal dialogue.

As you begin to add dialogue into your stories, start with character dialogue. That's the natural, easy-going dialogue that happens in the conversations and interactions between your characters. As you feel comfortable, you can dive deeper and begin to add inner dialogue. This will give additional insight and context to your stories. And then when you are ready to try an advanced technique, you can experiment with audience dialogue. Great storytelling effectively uses all three forms of dialogue.

DELIVERING DIALOGUE

Caution: When you first start adding dialogue to your stories, you can easily go overboard. I have seen many people who feel like they need to change their voice, add accents, and use other embellishments to deliver the line properly. But that usually isn't necessary. I feel like the best way to judge this is to record yourself and listen carefully to the playback, or videotape yourself and watch that to determine what works and what doesn't.

Ultimately, if it seems too theatric, it will feel awkward. The awkwardness often comes from trying things that are outside of your ability. For example, I cannot do accents. If I were to try and add an accent it would be confusing and distracting. So instead of changing my voice completely to deliver lines, I try to be subtle and simply change my tone. In the 4C story, when the jerk in 4C speaks, I deliver his lines with a serious and mean tone, but not with a different accent or voice. I would always err on the side of being subtle rather than over the top. With lines that carry great emotion, change the tone of your voice so you deliver the line with impact and the audience will realize just by the sound that you're expressing something important.

Most of the time I wouldn't recommend taking on a woman's voice if you are a man or a man's voice if you are a woman. But, again, the best way to judge for yourself is by recording your delivery and then asking: "Does this add to or take away from the story?"

When employing dialogue of any form, it's important to make sure that the audience knows who is talking, and who they are talking to. This can be accomplished in one of two ways: by narration, or by adding the recipient's name in the dialogue. In narrative form, you would say, "and he looked at Joe and said," before delivering the line. You set it up as the narrator so the audience obviously knows who is talking and who they are talking to. On the other hand, if you were using dialogue form to deliver the conversation, you would say, "and he looked at him and said, 'Joe, you know this …'" Either way allows the audience to understand exactly who is talking and who they are talking to.

Used artfully, dialogue brings your characters to life, adds humor and impact, and helps the audience truly relive and feel your story. In your storytelling bag of skills, there is no finer tool.

DETAILS

The second "D" that makes stories dynamic is Details.

In *The Story Factor,* Annette Simmons taught, "The counter-intuitive secret that all good storytellers understand is that the more specific the details, the more universal the connections." Details bring your stories to life and make it easier for the audience to paint a clear mental picture. The skill is knowing what details to present, and how to present them simply and quickly. You want to deliver details, but in as few words as possible. Be descriptive but not over-descriptive.

Again, remember the rule I introduced in Chapter 5: If it is not necessary to say, it becomes necessary not to say. This rule would seem to contradict the idea of adding details into your story, but they work together when you understand the areas where you want to use details and in what proportion.

LAT

Details in your stories fall into three main areas. To better remember them, the acronym is LAT.

- L – Location
- A – Amount
- T – Time

Understanding these three specific areas helps me to know where I should use details and where I should leave them out.

Let's examine the three areas one at a time.

Location—you don't want to just say "I met her in a hotel in Las Vegas." That paints a little bit of a picture, but you will paint a picture so much clearer if you say something like, "we met in room 302 at Caesars Palace in Las Vegas." Think about those details, are they distracting? No, they are very succinct—room 302 at Caesars Palace in Las Vegas. The reason I would contend a detail like that is important is because most people have a pretty good idea in general what Caesars Palace looks like, even if they haven't been there, so it creates more of an image and brings the stage you're setting to life. We think in terms of pictures and by saying the number 302, you've probably generated in your audience's mind a door with the number 302 on it. With location you want to be specific. That's why in the 4C story I use 4B and 4C. I don't just say I was sitting in first class and the man thought that I was in his seat but he was really in the seat across the aisle. There is just not the same impact in that. People can picture 4B and 4C. They will remember those numbers. It's funny because any time I get upgraded now and I sit in seat 4C, I will put that on Facebook by simply saying, "I'm in 4C on my flight today!" And that story is memorable enough that I will usually have 15, 20, 30 people that will like it or make a comment or say, wow, I love that story. That only happened because when I told the story I was specific about the location. It makes it memorable.

Amount—If there's a quantity, give it. Whether it's weight or size or dimension, if there's a way it can be measured, give that in your description. To illustrate why using details in amounts works, I want to share with you the story of Mel Fisher, the treasure hunter that I talked about earlier in this chapter.

EXPERT EXAMPLE:

The Mel Fisher story is a great example of how details make a story dynamic. You can watch me tell the Mel Fisher Story by using this link or you can read the story below. - bit.ly/163RUII

One of the best examples of commitment is that of Mel Fisher, the most successful treasure hunter the world has ever known.

Mel Fisher was born in Hobart, Indiana, in 1922. After serving in World War II he moved to California and bought a chicken farm. It was there that Mel found the two loves of his life: his wife Dolores, who he called Deo, and diving. In 1953 Mel and Deo were married and they sold the chicken farm, moved to Redondo Beach, and opened up the state's first dive shop.

Mel's aqua shop wasn't much but it was the only place for divers to get their gear. He and Deo offered free dive lessons to anyone who bought equipment. Determined to develop the sport, Mel modified existing equipment and snorkel gear to make it easier to use. The Fishers also made some of the first underwater films, showing people the glories of the ocean.

At one point, to gain publicity, Deo even challenged the women's record for staying underwater—50 hours. On August 2, 1959, when she was just 23 years old, Deo descended into an empty porpoise tank at the Hermosa Beach Aquarium with onlookers and film crews watching. For 55 hours, 37 minutes and 11 seconds she remained underwater, drinking juice and soup. To pass the time, she played chess with Mel, watched a TV he had set up outside the tank, and read soggy books and magazines.

Around the same time, Mel began diving on shipwrecks and soon discovered a passion for historic salvage and treasure hunting. Mel and Deo dove throughout the Caribbean and South America making movies and exploring the underwater world.

Hearing of a treasure fleet from 1715 that sank off of the coast of Florida, the Fishers made a decision to close their shop, move to Florida, and look for treasure full time. Not too long into their search, they uncovered a carpet of gold coins on the seabed. This was the first of several breathtaking discoveries by the Fishers. The finds spurred a "gold rush" of other treasure hunters to the site, forcing the State of Florida to write legislation governing the discovery and division of treasure in its waters. Included in the legislation was the fact that the state of Florida would receive 25 percent of any treasure found in its waters.

In 1968, Mel and Deo were looking for other places to dive, having found much of the 1715 fleet. It was then that a friend gave them a copy of Potter's, The Treasure Diver's Guide, in which the Nuestra Señora del Atocha was described as one of the richest shipwrecks ever lost. According to the guide, the Atocha had wrecked near the top of the Florida Keys, and once again, for Mel, the search was on.

Mel and his team searched the ocean floor everyday for three years without finding anything from the Atocha. Then in 1971, one of the divers found a gold chain 8 ½ feet long. The find kept them going, but it wasn't until two years later that Mel's son Kane found a single silver bar, with numbers inscribed on it that matched the Spanish manifest of the Atocha.

On July 13, 1975, after seven years of searching, Mel's oldest son Dirk found 5 bronze cannons from the Atocha.

Everyone thought the "Motherlode" was close, but a week later tragedy struck. One of their boats, The Northwind, capsized during the night and Dirk, his wife Angel, and diver Rick Gage were lost. In all, the hunt for the Atocha claimed four young lives, but the search continued, as Dirk would have wanted.

Mel Fisher always believed in success. He knew they would find the treasure of the Atocha, and he just kept going. His famous saying, "Today is the Day," reinforced an upbeat and optimistic outlook. His perseverance was almost inhuman. He searched the ocean floor everyday for more than a decade. He endured the loss of his son, daughter-in-law, and two of his other divers. He constantly convinced investors to buy into the dream so that he could continue to finance the search. And he relentlessly fought in court for seven years, through 141 court appearances, until finally the supreme court of Florida ruled in his favor and allowed him to keep all of the treasure he found.

Mel Fisher epitomizes what commitment is all about. And more importantly for him, it paid off. On July 20, 1985, after nearly 17 years of daily searching the ocean floor, a magnetometer contact indicated a large target on the seabed. Two divers went down to investigate, and found they were sitting on an entire reef of silver bars! They had finally found the Motherlode!

As news spread around Key West, everyone came out to the site to see what Mel had found. Even Jimmy Buffett dove down and sat on the pile of treasure.

All in all, Mel Fisher and his team found 127,000 silver coins, more than 900 silver bars averaging nearly 70 pounds apiece, more than 700 high quality emeralds and roughly 2,500 lighter stones, over 250 pounds of gold bars, discs, bits, and lengths of heavy gold chain, and hundreds of items of jewelry, silverware, crucifixes, and gold coins.

Estimates put the wrecks' value around $400 million. Mel Fisher had done it! With a total commitment, persisting for years and years, he had realized his dream.

BREAKING DOWN THE MEL FISHER STORY

The Mel Fisher story is a major struggle-to-solution

story. There are ups and there are downs and it builds to the climax where he finally finds the treasure of the Atocha, and when I give it, I want the audience to picture it because I'm using that story as an analogy for them to think about what they are going after. With that in mind, I don't just say he found it, I say he found the motherlode, the biggest treasure of all time, and I spell that out: 127,000 silver coins, more than 900 silver bars averaging nearly 70 pounds apiece, more than 700 high-quality emeralds and roughly 2,500 lighter stones, over 250 pounds of gold bars, discs, bits, and lengths of heavy gold chain, and hundreds of items of jewelry, silverware, crucifixes, and gold coins. Estimates put the wrecks' value around $400 million.

Don't those details bring it to life? Can you picture it? Can you imagine holding it in your hands? It's huge. It's impressive. What does 250 pounds of gold look like to you? What does 900 silver bars look like to you? What does 2,500 other gems look like to you? The detail paints a dynamic picture.

Time—When it comes to time, details are especially important. Don't just say I woke up early. Say "I woke up at 5 am this morning, I couldn't sleep any more." Adding that element of time doesn't take away from the story, it adds to it. In the Mel Fisher story, Deo set the world record by staying under water for 55 hours, 37 minutes and 11 seconds. Those numbers make the record sound impressive. That's what details do.

When it comes to location, when it comes to amount, and when it comes to time, the vividness is in the details. The balance is to be descriptive but not distracting. Add details in as few words as possible, but add them. It's your story's details that will help create universal connections, allow your audience to picture your story, and make it so much more dynamic.

THE TWO M'S THAT MAKE STORIES MEMORABLE

Chapter 10

THE TWO M'S THAT MAKE STORIES MEMORABLE

> "Storytelling reveals meaning without committing the error of defining it."
> – Hannah Arendt, German Political Philosopher

We see and we remember in images. When we hear a word or a phrase, our brains automatically attach a picture to it either from a previous physical experience or from our imagination. If I talk to you about butterflies, your mind will reflexively conjure up an image of a butterfly. If I talk about flying to the moon, some sort of mental picture of outer space will flash through your mind. It's a process as natural as breathing. And since our goal as storytellers is to present an influential message that is instantly recognizable and memorable, it's vital that we tap into that natural process and conjure up for our audience the most specific and vivid images possible. The way to do that is to brush every story with the twin M's: Movement and Metaphor.

MOVEMENT

> "If you tell me, it's an essay. If you show me, it's a story."
> – Barbara Greene

Movement in storytelling is an advanced technique. Executed properly, it renders a story eminently memorable. But it requires attention and practice. As with dialogue, the idea is to be subtle. Movement can be very easily overdone, and remember, storytelling is not theater and it's not drama. It's the story that's on stage, not the performance. Our storytelling movements should be natural and controlled, never taking over and detracting from the concept the story is extolling.

When I talk about movement, I'm talking about four specific areas:

1. Gestures—what you do with your hands.
2. Facial expressions—what you do with your face.
3. Posture—the way you position your body.
4. Motion—the way you move around a stage.

Let's look at the fundamentals of each area.

Gestures. Your hand motions should be simple and look natural. Pointing may be a great place to start when contemplating the use of gestures. When I tell the story about my mom and the galvanic spa, when I get to the part about her legs, my sister says, "What the heck is wrong with your legs?" With that line, she doesn't have a gesture—because I don't give her one. But when my mom then asks, "what do you mean?" and my sister answers, "That one has dimples and that one doesn't," I point to one leg and then the other leg, because that's a very natural gesture. It has a purpose to it and it enhances the story. As another example using pointing as a gesture, when I tell the 4C story and the man reveals that his seat is in 4C, I visibly point and say, "your seat is over there," Again, very natural, very authentic, very in context. The pointing adds to the story and helps people visualize it.

Now think about these natural gestures. If someone in

your story is reaching up for something, you can reach up as you tell the story. Or you can reach down for something. It sounds simple, I know, but it can make a big difference in effective storytelling. There are lots of little natural gestures that you can do with your hands that are going to bring your story to life and make it more memorable. If you're talking about picking up stones, you can reach out and grab an imaginary stone. If you're talking about skipping rocks, you can make that motion. Such movements cement that image and the story it's a part of, in the mind of your audience.

Facial Expressions. A lot can be said with your face. Without uttering a word, you can show excitement, you can show shock, you can show sadness, worry, annoyance, anticipation, and all sorts of different emotions. This will most often come into play as a complement to the dialogue between your characters. If you are shocked, give a shocked facial expression. In the 4C story there are times when my response to the jerk in 4C is rolling my eyes and making a face like I can't believe he just said that to me. I can say a lot with my facial expressions. Facial expressions make your characters come to life. You're not just delivering their lines, you're delivering their lines in real time with real motion and emotion.

Posture. The way you position and move your body speaks volumes. Again, this type of movement needs to be subtle. Less is usually more. You don't have to dramatically change positions, turn as if you're speaking to the other person, or move back and forth between characters. Body language is best expressed with restraint. For example, in the 4C story, the man is standing in the aisle when he confronts me about being in his seat. So, as I relate that part of the story, I simply look up. And as he delivers his lines, I simply look down—effectively communicating with my posture that he's standing and I'm sitting.

Motion. The fourth area of movement is motion. It involves walking around, changing places, creating motion. With few exceptions, it is to be used in a story only when the audience is large enough. In one-on-one situations, there are very few times it will be natural enough to be effective.

Let me give you an example of the effectiveness of motion in storytelling. I was in San Antonio, Texas, at an event not long ago and there was another speaker there. He told a story and used motion in a way that was fantastic. It really brought the story to life. He was talking about his store that he owned in Hawaii in the 80's and there was this craze over yo-yo's. He said there would be a line that went out of the store and around the corner. When he said this, he moved from one spot on the stage that he had created as the door to his store and walked and turned the corner to where the end of the line would be. The audience could visualize what he was describing because he created the scene with his motion on stage. Then he went on to relate how tourists as they were walking by would stop and talk to people in line. In doing so, he remembered where the place was that he had created for the line and walked there. That's important when you use motion on a stage— you want to create places that you're going to go back to as the story flows. It won't work if you just randomly choose a different place for the end of the line—it needs to be the exact same spot. He talked about how these tourists would walk up to the line and ask, "What are people standing in line for?" And the people in the line would say, "yo-yo's." Then he said, "The tourists would shrug their shoulders, walk to the end of the line and get in line too." As he said that, he literally walked, turned the corner, stopped, turned again, folded his arms, and took his place at the end of the line. It was extremely effective.

The motion he created in telling that story completely brought it to life.

On a stage, we call motion an act out. This is where you have a chance to act out certain pieces of your story by adding motion that can make it funny, visually engaging, and memorable.

Expert Tip: To see a great example of motion in a story, click on the link to see my friend Les Brown tell one of his signature stories. bit.ly/13gX9ac

PERFECTING MOVEMENT

In each of the four areas of motion, I recommend that you videotape your speeches so you can play them back in private and review and assess your movements. There is no better feedback. Obviously, if you just tape record yourself you can't get the important visual replay. Storytelling starts with content and delivery, and once you have that part mastered and you are ready to take it up a notch, you can look at the gestures, the facial expressions, the posture, and the way you move around the stage to improve your delivery and impact.

For me personally, as a speaker, this has become my main area of emphasis. As I analyze video of my presentations, I am working to perfect the movement in my storytelling because I think it sets great speakers apart from the rest.

I would suggest that in your first review of your videotape that you pay attention to your natural movement—the unconscious way that you move. Movement should be natural and needs to add to the story. If it creates a better image in the mind of your audience and it makes your story more memorable, then you are on the right track. If it is distracting, then take it out. Once you can recognize the natural-looking movements that are effective for you, you can begin to tweak them and make them even more impactful.

Also, take care to pay close attention to the dialogue in your story because most of the movement is going to pertain to the characters you bring to life. As you look at the characters in your story, analyze and determine what movements can best bring out their personalities.

Another way to analyze movement is by watching the

video in mute. Without sound, you can focus on the movement and see what story you are telling with your hands, face, and body. This will put you in the frame of mind of your most visual learners and see how you can make the story more visually stimulating.

The last thing to think about is the size of your audience because your movement will grow or diminish accordingly. The smaller the group, the smaller the gestures. Let your movement grow as the audience grows. With practice, you'll be able to feel the right amount of movement for each size of audience. When you're in tune with your audience, and when you're using all the storytelling techniques that we've discussed, you can gain a good sense when your movements feel awkward or appropriate. Always be in tune with your audience and you'll be able to adjust your movements accordingly.

METAPHORS

"The charismatic communicators take the complex and make it simple, and the simple and make it meaningful. They do that with stories and metaphors"
—Fortune Magazine

When I refer to metaphors—the second M that makes stories memorable—I am talking about an analogy between two objects or ideas that are otherwise unlike entities. Metaphors are used to compare the known to the unknown. If you want to get technical, we could define symbolism, simile, and parallels, but for our purposes as storytellers they are essentially one and the same and we'll put them all in the category of metaphor.

We often speak metaphorically. Have you ever said "as cold as ice," "a train wreck waiting to happen," "comparing apples and oranges?" Metaphors all. We routinely sprinkle our everyday conversations with metaphors, they help us to be understood and they help us to relate. In storytelling, their power only increases in helping make the unknown known and the intangible tangible.

One type of metaphor may be an object lesson. An object lesson that I use when I speak about leadership is to have the audience raise their right hands. I tell them to take their pointer finger and their thumb and make a circle, like it's an "okay" sign, and then I say, "Now do as I'm doing and slowly bring that circle down and put it on your cheek." But as I say "cheek," I take my hand and put it on my chin. And then I say, "Look around—how many of you put it on your chin?" Invariably, the majority of people will do exactly what I do, not what I say. That then becomes a metaphor to teach the concept that actions speak louder than words.

Metaphors help people see so much clearer because they can relate. The concept you are presenting suddenly comes into sharp focus because it can be easily compared to something already familiar to them. It is like a magic ingredient in your story.

I started as an entrepreneur when I was 21 years old. And one of the challenges that I faced in getting my business going was establishing credibility with people because of my age—or, more accurately, my lack of age. I tried several different ways to overcome the perception that I was too young to be taken seriously. What ultimately worked best was a metaphor-based story I developed. When I sat down with people who clearly had a bias against me because of my youth, I'd start off by saying, "You know, it's interesting as I'm talking to you because I know some people look at me and they think what does this guy know about business? He's young, He's 21. He really doesn't have a ton of experience. But you know, I kind of feel like a young Bill Gates." And when I put it that way, most of the time they would smile and then I'd say, "What I mean is, you know, Bill Gates was 19 years old when he started Microsoft. He dropped out of college and he had this vision, he told everyone that he was going to take computers, which were the size of refrigerators, and he was going to put one in every house in the world. People probably thought he was nuts. Who was this young, naïve entrepreneur?"

Then I'd continue: "Now, I'm not saying that I'm going to change the world, and I'm not saying that I'm going to make as much money as Bill Gates. What I am saying is that I have something here and I know where I'm going with this, and I want you to really sit down and take a look at it. Are you willing to do that?"

That metaphor-based story worked like magic to establish credibility. I compared myself, an unknown entrepreneur, to a known entrepreneur, Bill Gates, and that little story caused people to forget about my age and concentrate on our product. Eventually we ended up building an incredibly successful business.

Another metaphor that I use in the form of a story is when

I speak to high school students. One of the messages of my leadership speech is the importance of who you hang out with. To illustrate this point, I share a metaphor-based story about monkeys.

Expert Example: You can read the monkey story or watch me tell it at the link below. bit.ly/WPWlQk

Four monkeys were placed in a room that had a tall pole in the center. Suspended from the top of that pole was a bunch of bananas. One of the hungry monkeys started climbing the pole to get something to eat, but just as he reached out to grab a banana, he was doused with a bucket of cold water. Squealing, he scampered down the pole and abandoned his attempt to feed himself. Each monkey made a similar attempt, and each one was drenched with cold water. After making several attempts, they all finally gave up.

Then the researchers removed one of the monkeys from the room and replaced him with a new monkey. As the newcomer began to climb the pole, the other three grabbed him and pulled him down to the ground. After trying to climb the pole several times and being dragged down by the others, he finally gave up and never attempted to climb again.

The researchers replaced the original monkeys one by one, and each time a new monkey was brought in he would be dragged down by the others before he could reach the bananas. In time, the room was filled with monkeys who had never received a cold shower. However, none of them would climb the pole, and not one of them knew why.

What kind of person—monkeys—are you hanging out with? Do they build you up or tear you down?

In talking to teenagers, I don't want to just say it matters who you hang out with, because if you hang out with a bunch of losers, you become a loser. They've heard that before. But they haven't heard a study about a bunch of monkeys that they can see visually getting doused with water. As I give my speech to high school students, that's the number one thing that they comment on—the monkey story. It sticks it in their minds. Which is exactly why I use it.

FINDING METAPHORS

Metaphor-based stories are unbelievably powerful and memorable. So how do you find them? How do you develop good metaphors?

I've found that influencers are always aware. Just as they are constantly on the lookout for good stories and experiences that will motivate audiences, they are also constantly on the lookout for metaphors. They keep their eyes peeled for things that pop up, examples and parallels that could be extrapolated into a message, that they could use as a comparison, as an object lesson, as an effective way to teach a concept. Because of their awareness they are always finding great material for metaphors everywhere that they go.

I had a friend recently who was in traffic school and she sent me this text: "The judge just said it's a lot easier to give statements than it is to ask questions." That is the basis for a great story. Be aware—metaphors, like stories, are all around you.

As experiences happen, you want to constantly ask two questions:
1. What could this compare to?
2. What is the lesson in this?

You're always going to find material popping up if you just pay attention. It may come from books, experiences, movies, current events, or a multitude of other sources. Then, as you're developing your stories, or preparing a sales pitch or presentation, ask the two questions in reverse: What can this concept compare to? What's a good metaphor to reinforce this lesson? Your treasure trove of experiences will fill the needs of your presentation and create the kind of stories that will be memorable and carry great influence.

Remember the word's of Plato—"Those who tell the stories, rule the world"

Best of luck!

About The Author

More than one million people from 50 countries have learned from Ty Bennett's insights on Leadership, Entrepreneurship and Communication.

When Ty was 21 years old he started a business with his brother Scott, which they built to over $20 million in annual revenue while still in their twenties.

Ty was recently featured in Utah Business' Top 40 Under 40. Ty currently sits on several boards, including two non-profits, including serving as the President of The Mountain West chapter of The National Speakers Association.

Ty is a sought after keynote speaker as well as speech/presentation coach. As a speaker Ty is a young, fresh voice with a fun, engaging style. Ty has shared the stage with celebrities, world renowned thought leaders and recently with President Bush and President Clinton.

Ty is the author of The Power of Influence as well as the video training program, Facts Tell, Stories Sell. Ty lives in Utah with his wife Sarah, daughter Andie, and sons Tanner and Drew.

To learn more about Ty Bennett – visit www.leadershipinc.com